A SHORT
GEOGRAPHY OF BENGAL

A SHORT
GEOGRAPHY OF BENGAL

W.H. ARDEN WOOD

GYAN

Published by

Gyan Publishing House
5, Ansari Road
Daryaganj, New Delhi-110002
Phone: 011-47034999, 9811692060
E-mail: books@gyanbooks.com

Distribution Network
gyanbooks.com
India, USA, Canada, UK, Australia

ISBN: 978-93-6780-039-3 (PB)
First Published, 1895

2nd Impression 2024

Printed at: Gyan Press, Delhi.

A SHORT GEOGRAPHY OF BENGAL
Author: W.H. ARDEN WOOD

A SHORT GEOGRAPHY OF BENGAL.

PHYSICAL FEATURES
of
BENGAL
Scale of Miles
0 50 100 150
Gogra R.
Gandak R.
Ganges R.
Kusi R.
Darjeeling
Ganges R.
Hazaribagh
Dacca
Megna R.
CHOTA NAGPUR
CALCUTTA
Chittagong
Hooghly R.
BAY
of
BENGAL

A SHORT
GEOGRAPHY OF BENGAL

BY

ARDEN WOOD, B.A., F.C.S.,

:ipal of La Martinière College, Calcutta; Examiner to the
Calcutta and the Punjab Universities.

WITH MAPS AND ILLUSTRATIONS.

LONDON
GEORGE BELL & SONS
AND BOMBAY
1895

CONTENTS.

PART I.—GENERAL VIEW OF THE PROVINCE.

SECTION		PAGE
1.	Name	1
2.	Geographical Position	2
3.	Divisions of the Province	3
4.	Size	5
5.	General Surface Features	6
6.	River System	9
7.	Climate	28
8.	Plants and Animals	32
9.	Population	35
10.	Products, Industries, Commerce	37
11.	Internal Communications	39

PART II.—GEOGRAPHY OF THE DIVISIONS.

BENGAL PROPER.

PAGE

I. Presidency Division 43

II. Burdwān Division 61

III. Rājshāhi Division 73

IV. Dācca Division 89

V. Chittagong Division . . . 90

BIHĀR.

I. Patna Division 111

II. Bhāgalpur Division . . . 131

ORISSA.

I. Orissa Division 145

II. The Tributary States . . . 156

CHOTA NĀGPUR.

I. Chota Nāgpur Division . . . 169

II. Nine Tributary States . . . 170

MAPS AND ILLUSTRATIONS.

PAGE

Physical Features of Bengal *Map (front)*

Bengal Presidency . . . . *Map* xiv

Bengal showing Adjacent Territories, *Map* 2

Formation of "Chars" 11

Section of River-bed 12

Fluvial Action of Bhāgirathi . . . 13

Formation of Bīls or Jhīls . . . 13

Change in the Course of the Ganges . 16

Gangetic River System in 18th Century and now 18

Section of Delta 20

Presidency Division . . . . *Map* 44

The Hooghly, at Calcutta 49

Hindu Temple 56

Burdwān Division . . . . . *Map* 60

The Hooghly, near Chinsura . . . 70

		PAGE
RĀJSHĀHI DIVISION	*Map*	72
ELEPHANTS CROSSING THE TORSA . . .		79
SNOWY RANGE ABOVE DARJEELING . . .		85
DACCA DIVISION	*Map*	88
THE BURIGANGA AT DĀCCA (NAWAB'S PALACE)		96
CHITTAGONG DIVISION	*Map*	98
SCENE IN HILL TIPPERA		107
PATNA DIVISION	*Map*	112
SONEPUR FAIR		115
SONE CANAL		120
TEMPLES AT BUDDH GĀYA		123
OLD GĀYA		125
BHĀGALPUR DIVISION	*Map*	130
GANGES AND FORT MONGHYR		133
PROVINCE OF ORISSA	*Map*	144
TEMPLE AT JAGANNĀTH, PURI		155
CHOTA NĀGPUR PROVINCE	*Map*	162

PREFACE.

My chief obligations in writing this little book have been to the *Statistical Account of Bengal*, and the *Imperial Gazetteer of India*, edited by Sir W. W. Hunter; the *Census Report of 1891*; the *Bengal Administration Report for 1892-3*; and the various maps published by the Surveyor-General of India. I have also made use of *Rennell's Atlas*, *Hamilton's Hindostan*; *Hooker's Himalayan Journals*, and other works. Hooker's delightful book—the journal of a traveller who went leisurely through the country by river and road—is, I fear, likely to be the last of its kind as regards Bengal. I know no book which gives the general reader so just and distinct an impression of the parts of Bengal which it describes; and the writer, in his travels, saw something of every Division of the Presidency except Orissa.

Bengal is a land of great fluvial action, and its river geography is constantly changing. The consequence is that existing maps, which are all based on a survey made a number of years ago, are inevitably, in many respects, inaccurate. Recent information has, however, enabled me to introduce various corrections in the maps given here.

The illustrations are from photographs, and I have to thank the photographers, both amateur and professional, who have been so good as to send me their productions to select from.

A note on nomenclature may be useful to English readers. The proper names of Bengal geography, like most other proper names, have a meaning, though it is often obscured by the popular, or by the English, form of the word. In the following examples of river names, however, it is plain enough: Mahānadi (great river), Mahānanda (great joy), Gumti (winding), Brahmaputra (son of Brahma), Noboganga (new Ganga or Ganges), Subarnarekha (thread of gold), and in many other instances. In place names certain terminations, analogous to the English *—ton*, *—ham*, *—by*, are very common. Such are *—ganj* (mart), *—hāt* (open-air market), *—ghāt* (steps leading to a bathing place, and hence, the bathing place itself),*—ābād* (cultivated area), *—nagar* (city), *—pur* (city), as seen in Revelganj, Bāgerhāt, Rānāghāt, Murshidābād, Krishnagar, Rangpur.

The spelling of the proper names is that of the Bengal spelling-list. This retains the old spelling where it has obtained a literary currency, as in Calcutta, Hooghly, Cuttack, Buxār, Burdwān, etc. In other cases a system of transliteration is adopted which approximately represents the correct pronunciation if the vowels are given the values indicated in the following list.

ā, the sound of *a* in f*a*ther: Sāra, Bānkura.
a, the sound of *a* in wom*a*n: Katwa, Baxa.
e, the vowel sound in fray: Keshpur.
ī, the sound of *ee* in f*ee*l: Bīrbhum.
i, the sound of *i* in p*i*ll: Siwān.
o, the sound of *o* in c*o*-exist: Nator.
u, the sound of *oo* in p*oo*l: Khulna, Puri,
g, is always hard; and *h* is an aspirate in such combinations as *bh*, *dh*, *gh*, *kh*, *jh*, *ph*, *th*.
ch is sounded as in church; *sh* as in shawl.

W. H. A. W.

Castleton, Darjeeling,
April, 1895.

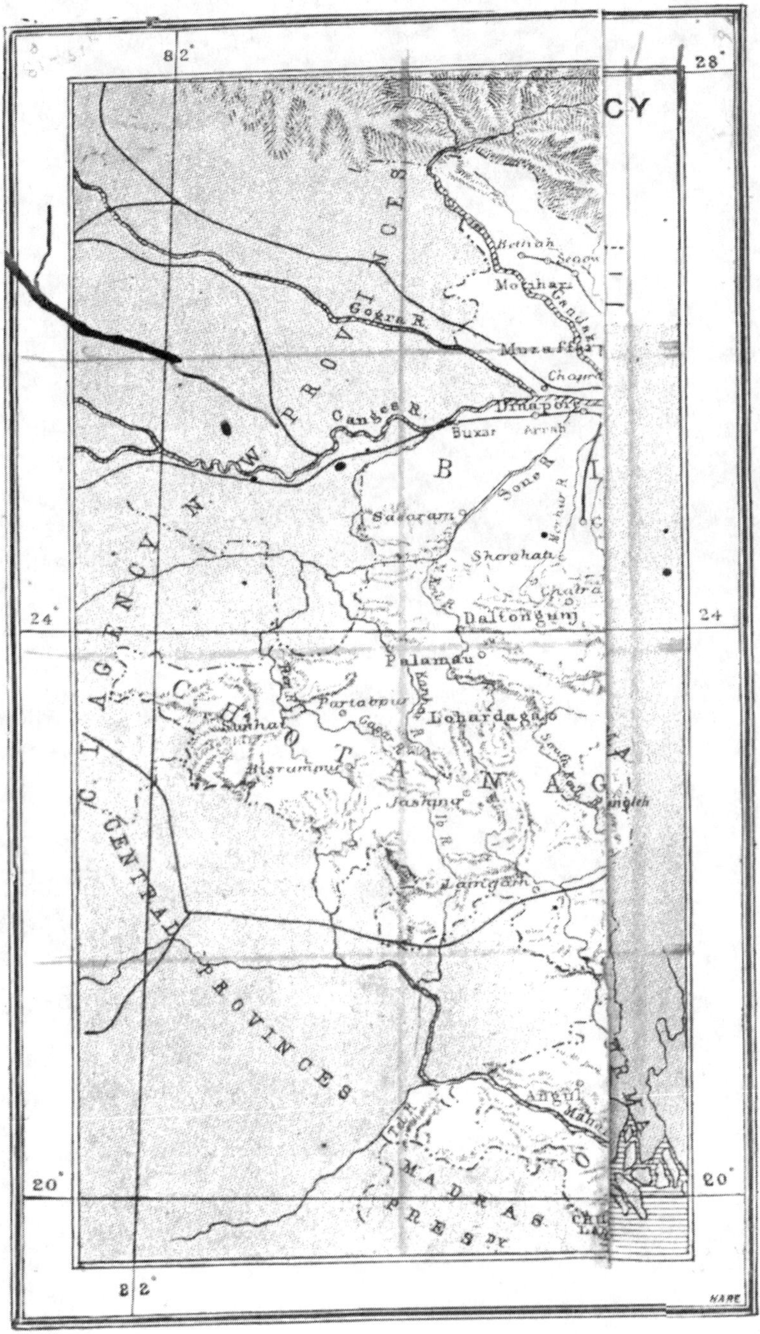

82°
28°
CY
Bettiah
Motihari
Gogra R.
Muzaffar
Ganges R.
Dinapore
Buxar
Arrah
B
Sone R.
Sasaram
Sherghati
Daltongunj
24°
24
Palamau
Partabpur
Lohardaga
Sunhat
Bisrampur
Jashpur
Angul
20°
20°
CENTRAL PROVINCES
MADRAS PRES^DY
82°
HARE

GEOGRAPHY OF BENGAL.

PART I.—GENERAL VIEW OF THE PROVINCE.

NAME.

THE name **Bengal** originally applied to the deltas of the Ganges and Brahmaputra, and a portion of the plains to the north, and this is still the application of the name as used by the people of the country., But after the establishment of the English power in India, the name was used much more loosely. The early factories of the East India Company in north-eastern India were all regarded as being in Bengal, and the application of the name extended with the influence of the Company, until the official designation, "The Presidency of Fort William in Bengal," covered, not only Bihār and Orissa, but the whole of the British conquests in northern India. In the end, however, the unwieldy size of the Bengal Presidency rendered its sub-division necessary, and the application of the name was again narrowed. *Bengal*, as one of the eight great provinces into which India under British administration is now divided, is made up of the territories which constitute the Lieutenant-Governorship of Bengal, and the Native States which are in political dependence upon that Government.

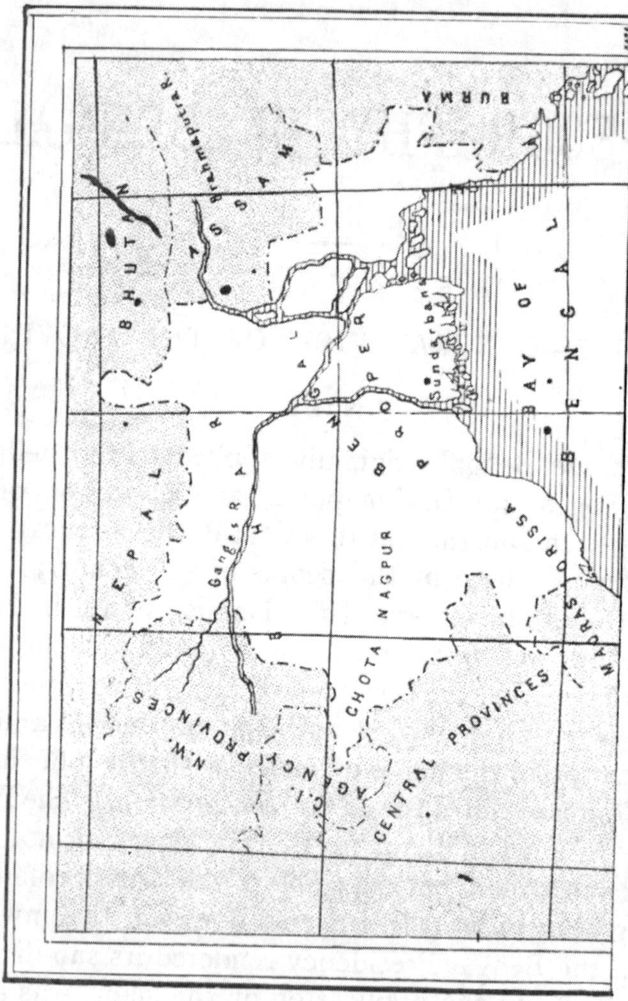

MAP OF BENGAL, SHOWING ADJACENT TERRITORIES.

GEOGRAPHICAL POSITION.

The Province of Bengal, as thus constituted, is, on the whole, a compact territory. It lies at the head of the

Bay of Bengal, extending chiefly north and north-west from its coast-line, which runs from the river Nāf on the east side of the bay to the Chilka lake on the west side. The Province is situated partly within and partly without the tropics, being, roughly speaking, divided into two halves by the tropic of Cancer, and contained between 19° 28′ and 28° 9′ north latitude, and 81° 37′ and 93° 18′ east longitude. It is bounded on the north by Nepāl, Tibet, and Bhutān; on the east by the British Provinces of Assam and Burmah; on the south by the Bay of Bengal and the Madras Presidency; on the west by the Central Provinces, the States of the Central India Agency, and the North-West Provinces.

Divisions of the Province.

Bengal is divided into four sub-provinces: *Bengal Proper*, *Bihār*, *Orissa*, and *Chota Nāgpur*. This division of the country has no political significance. It is rather a historical division, and, as it happens, it corresponds very fairly with a division of the country according to its natural characters. *Bengal Proper* is practically the Bengal of ancient times: the country known as Bengal by the natives of India, where the Bengāli language is spoken. *Orissa* and *Bihār* were distinct provinces under Muhammedan rule, and, in still earlier times, formed parts of Hindu kingdoms. Uriya and Hindi are the respective vernaculars of these provinces. *Chota Nāgpur*, inhabited by wild hill-tribes of aboriginal race, was outside the pale of the ancient civilisation of the country.

At the present day the whole country directly under British rule is divided into *Districts*, each of which has its administrative officials. Several

Districts grouped together form a *Division*, which is in charge of a Commissioner, who is directly responsible to the Lieutenant-Governor of the Province. The following list gives the nine Divisions or Commissionerships into which Bengal is divided, together with the Districts of each Division. The Native States are classed under the Division with which they are geographically and politically associated.

I. BENGAL PROPER.

1. *Presidency Division.*
   Districts: Calcutta. 24-Parganas. Nadia. Murshidābād. Jessore. Khulna.

2. *Burdwān Division.*
   Districts: Burdwān. Bānkura. Bīrbhum. Midnapore. Hooghly. Howrah.

3. *Rājshāhi Division.*
   Districts: Rājshāhi. Dinājpur. Jalpāiguri. Darjeeling. Rangpur. Bogra. Pabna.
   Native States: Kuch Bihār. Sikkim.

4. *Dācca Division.*
   Districts: Dācca. Mymensingh. Faridpur. Bāckergunge.

5. *Chittagong Division.*
   Districts: Tippera. Noākhāli. Chittagong. South Lushāi Hills.
   Native State: Hill Tippera.

II.—BIHĀR.

1. *Patna Division.*

Districts: Patna. Gāya. Shāhābād. Darbhanga. Muzaffarpur. Sāran. Champāran.

2. *Bhāgalpur Division.*

Districts: Bhāgalpur. Monghyr. Purnea. Mālda. Sonthāl Parganas.

III.—ORISSA.

1. *Orissa Division.*

Districts: Balasore. Cuttack. Puri. Angul and Khondmāls.

Native States: Seventeen Tributary States.

IV.—CHOTA NĀGPUR.

1. *Chota Nāgpur Division.*

Districts: Hazāribāgh. Lohārdaga. Palāmau. Mānbhum. Singhbhum.

Native States: Nine Tributary States.

SIZE.

The total area of the Province is estimated at 197,651 square miles. The surveyed portion under British rule is 151,535 square miles; to this must be added the area of the Sundarbans, hitherto unsurveyed, but estimated at 5,309 square miles, and the area of the recently annexed South Lushāi District, also unsurveyed, but estimated at 2,400 square miles; giving as the total area under direct British administration, 159,244 square miles. The area of the Native States: Sikkim, Kuch Bihār, Hill Tippera, the Tributary States of Orissa and Chota Nāgpur is estimated at 38,407 square miles.

The Province of Bengal is the largest of the political divisions of India; the next to it, in point of size, being Burma, with an area of 171,430 square miles. Of European states, Spain, with an area of 197,670 square miles, is almost the same size; France, with an area of 204,092 square miles, is somewhat larger; while the United Kingdom, with an area of 120,973 square miles, is considerably smaller.

The length of the Province from east to west along the Tropic of Cancer is about 650 miles: from the north of Sikkim to the Chilka Lake, about 640 miles; and its greatest length, from near Tribeni Ghāt on the borders of Nepāl in the north-west, to the river Nāf, in Chittagong in the south-east, 708 miles.

General Surface Features.

The coast of Bengal is everywhere low, though in places protected by sandhills, and the country near the sea is liable to devastation by storm-waves. The land in the neighbourhood of the numerous channels by which the rivers make their way into the sea is very low, often barely above high-water mark. It is generally swampy and covered with dense jungle, uninhabited except by tigers and other wild animals. The best known example of such country is the Sundarbans.

More than one-half of Bengal consists of alluvial plain formed of silt which has been brought down by the great rivers. Throughout this portion of the province, except where we approach the hills, nothing so coarse as gravel is found; the ground to a great depth consists of sand, clay, and like materials; and the surface, wherever it is flooded during the rainy season, constantly receives fresh deposits of mud which render the soil of inexhaustible fertility. The "plains," as this low country is called, comprise (1) the flat country traversed by the Ganges and Brahmaputra and their tributaries before the commencement of the delta; (2) the combined deltas of these two great rivers; (3) the strip of alluvial land between the Orissa hills and the coast on the west side of the Bay of Bengal; (4) a similar but smaller strip between the Chittagong hills and the coast on the east side of the Bay.

In all these tracts the land rises very gradually as we go up the rivers. In many parts of the Gangetic delta the level of the country is less than 20 feet above sea level at a distance of 100 miles from the sea; and only at its very highest does it reach 100 feet. In fact the rise is very gradual all along the Ganges, and at the point where the river enters the Province, more than 300 miles from the sea, the general level of the country is still below 200 feet. Going north from the Ganges towards the Himalaya there is no marked increase of elevation until about 30 miles from the hills, and then the plains somewhat suddenly rise to near 300 feet, and remain at about this elevation until we reach the hills. South of the Ganges, and west of the delta, the plains are of less extent, and soon begin to rise in undulations towards the hill country of Chota Nāgpur and Orissa. The hill country of Bengal, which forms rather more than a third of its total area, occupies three distinct parts of the Province:

(1) a portion of Northern Bengal and Sikkim, where it is part of the Himalaya; (2) the greater portion of Chota Nāgpur and Orissa; (3) Hill Tippera, and the eastern portion of Chittagong Division.

(1) Most of the northern frontier of Bengal runs some distance from the base of the hills. In the extreme north-west, however, it includes some low ranges bordering on Nepāl, and in the north-east of Purnea District it turns sharply north, ascends the outlying spurs of the great Singalīlā range, and follows it over successively greater heights to Kanchinjinga, 28,150 feet above the level of the sea. Somewhat north of Kanchinjinga the frontier turns east, and, after rounding Mount Donkhia, 23,176 feet, follows the Cholā range south to the lower hills abutting on the plains, and separating British territory from Bhutān. This northward projection of Bengal includes Sikkim and part of Darjeeling District, and is a confused mass of gigantic mountains. In Northern Sikkim heights of 20,000 feet and upwards, covered with perpetual snow, are numerous, and the frontier of Sikkim and Tibet seldom descends below the snow-line (about 16,000 feet).

(2) The hill country of Chota Nāgpur and Orissa is a northward and eastward continuation of the high land of Central India. It is not possible to trace any well-defined mountain system; the whole tract is a multitude of irregular ranges, sometimes crowding together about a culminating height, sometimes opening out to form wide valleys. These hills do not reach any great height. Peaks of over 2,000 feet are numerous, and a good number exceed 3,000 feet, especially in the west of Chota Nāgpur. The highest

of all is the well known Pārasnāth Hill, which rises from comparatively low-lying land to a height of 4,480 feet; but this is an outlying hill on the eastern border of Hazāribāgh District. Several small ranges rise out of the plains lying between Chota Nāgpur and the Ganges.' Most of these are outliers of the Chota Nāgpur system, but the most important of them, the Rājmahāl Hills, is an isolated range, having no geological connection with it.

(3) The hill country east of the Bay, in Hill Tippera and Chittagong, is a succession of long, narrow ranges, generally parallel to each other and the coast. They are sometimes joined by transverse ranges, or broken by transverse valleys. The outermost ranges are low, averaging under 1,000 feet; the ranges become higher towards the east, and in South Lushāi their average elevation exceeds 2,000 feet, while some peaks rise to 8,000 feet.

River System.

The river-system of Bengal is the most important feature of its physical geography. It affords examples of every type of river: from the glacier-fed stream which, in a course of about a hundred miles, rushes down through mountain gorges from 19,000 feet to the plains at a level of 300 feet, to the sluggish deltaic distributary, which meanders through mud and jungle to the sea. But the course of the rivers through the plains is what is of most importance, and the prosperity of the country is bound up with the network of streams which covers them.

The water of all Bengal rivers is laden with silt to a degree which varies with the season of the year and the special nature of the river. The latter depends on the length of its course, the velocity of its current, and the nature of the country through which it flows. The Brahmaputra, for instance, is said to bring down nearly twice as much silt as the Ganges; but, during the rainy season, every river is brown with the silt it carries.

The capacity of moving water to carry solid particles depends upon its velocity. The rapid mountain rivers bear along water-worn fragments of rock, and carry them out into the plains, but the larger fragments are soon dropped, and not even pebbles are found in the Himalayan streams thirty miles away from the hills. But a fall of five inches per mile is sufficient to enable a river not only to carry along the finer particles which constitute silt, but even to take up more on its journey through the plains; and the average fall of the Bengal rivers does not drop below this until near the head of the delta. Should, however, the current be checked from any cause, it becomes unable to carry the whole of its silt, which therefore begins to be deposited. This is what usually happens at the junction of two rivers. At the point of junction the two currents check one another, and form an area of comparatively still water. Here the silt deposits, and tends to build up a tongue of land separating the two rivers, and deferring the actual point of junction, which thus, in course of years, moves down stream.

A striking instance of this is the movement of the point of junction of the Ganges and Gogra. In the early part of the century Chapra and Revelganj were both on the Ganges below the junction. They are now on the Gogra some miles above it. The dangerous "James and Mary" sands in the Hooghly are caused by the check given to its current by the Dāmodar and

Rupnārāin rivers, which flow into it almost at right angles six miles apart. Between the entrances of these two rivers there is comparatively slack water, and here these shifting shoals are formed. In the last century, when the Dāmodar joined the Hooghly at a higher point of its course, these shoals were not nearly so dangerous. And the "bars" which usually obstruct the mouths of silt-bearing rivers are due to the deposition of silt and sand in the slack water where river and sea meet.

In the Bengal rivers quite trivial causes, such as a fallen tree, or a sunken boat, are sufficient to check the current, and bring about the deposition of silt. This then begins to build up a sand bank, which may form an island, or an accretion to one of the banks of the river. These formations are called *chars;* they are being constantly formed in every river of Bengal, and are one of the great causes of the changes of course which so frequently occur.

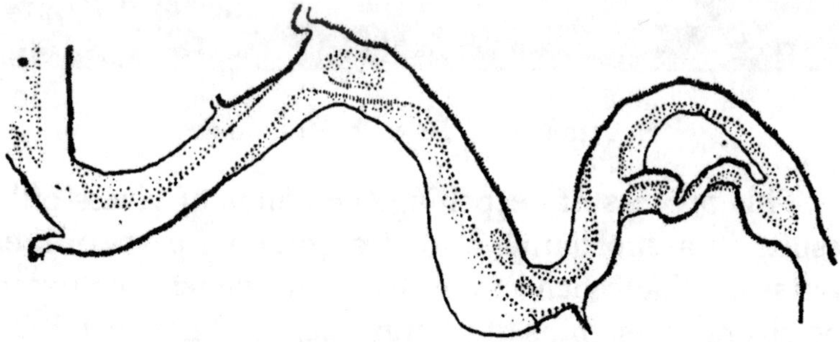

SECTION OF THE GANGES, ILLUSTRATING THE DEPOSITION OF SILT TO FORM "CHARS."

The counterpart of this process is equally common; namely, the destruction of land, and its removal in the shape of silt; and by suitably directing the current of a river, it may be made to cut away *chars*, and deepen its channel. This cutting action is, of course, being continually exerted upon the banks, which are usually composed of soft materials. Even supposing that the course of a river were, in any part, perfectly straight, with a current strongest in the middle, this state of things could not long continue. Some cause, probably trivial, would bring about a deflection of the current against one of the banks, which would speedily be cut away into a rapidly deepening curve. The strength of the current would follow the curve, and deepen the channel under the concave bank; silt would deposit in the slack water near the other bank; and before long we should reach the normal form of river in the plains: a winding channel, with a well-defined high bank on the outside of the bend, under which the deep water flows; the water gradually shallowing to the opposite bank, which is usually low and shelving.

SECTION OF A BENGAL RIVER-BED.

This process of deepening the bends of rivers often results in a shortening and straightening parts of their courses. Each bend away from the general course of the river corresponds to a return bend. These bends cut towards one another, and may, if the river is very winding, come so close together at some point that the river when in flood breaks across at the narrowest part. The portion of the channel thus deserted eventually becomes an isolated piece of still water, choked with weeds. Such pieces of water, generally highly-curved in shape, are common in the basins of rivers which traverse alluvial plains: in the basin of the Mississippi they are

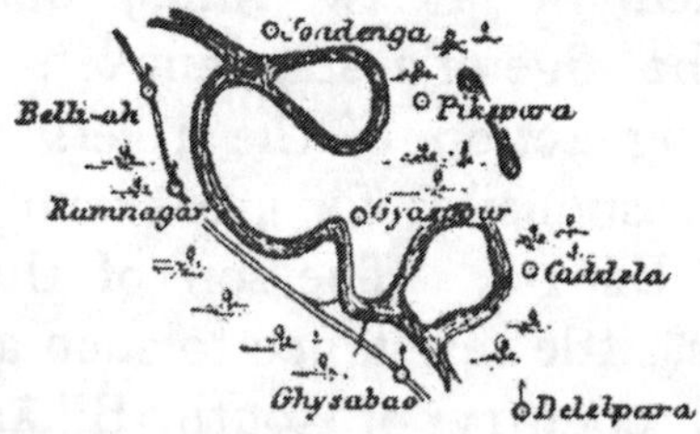

FROM RENNELL'S MAP OF COSSIMBUZAR ISLAND, ILLUSTRATING FLUVIAL ACTION OF THE BHĀGIRATHI.

called *bayous*; in Bengal, *bīls* (Bengāli), or *jhīls* (Hindi); but the same names, *bīl* or *jhīl*, are given to any permanent piece of shallow water in swampy low-lying ground, whether connected with a river or not.

One of the most striking instances of this kind of fluvial action is afforded by the ruin of Cossimbuzar,

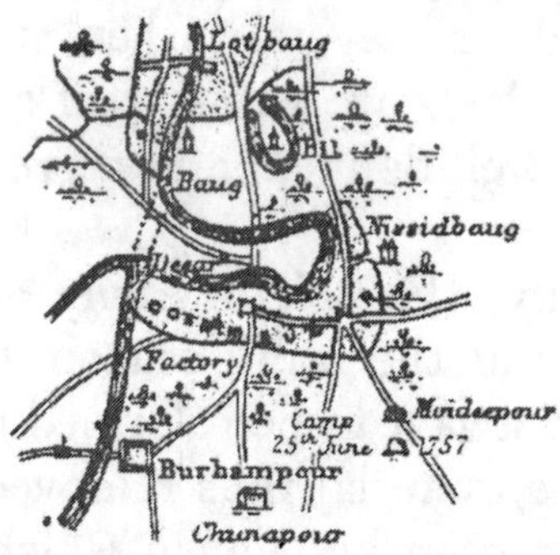

FROM RENNELL'S MAP, SHOWING THE COURSE OF THE BHĀGIRATHI BEFORE IT CUT ACROSS (AS SHOWN BY THE DOTTED LINE) AND DESERTED COSSIMBUZAR. THE EXTRACT ALSO SHOWS A BĪL, FORMED BY A PREVIOUS CHANGE IN THE COURSE OF THE RIVER.

one of the earliest and most important trade marts in Bengal. The factory was situated at the extremity of a deep bend of the Bhāgirathi near Murshidābād.

About 1813 the river broke across the neck of the bend, and left Cossimbuzar some miles to the east. The factory was necessarily abandoned, and its site is now marked by a few ruins, buried in jungle, standing on the edge of a stagnant *bīl*.

This cutting action of the rivers works in other ways, and is responsible for great changes in the river geography of Bengal. The soil of the plains offers, in most places, little resistance to such action. Except near the hill country of south Bihār and western Bengal no rock is found; and the presence of harder constituents in the soil has set a limit to the southward movement of the channel of the Ganges, and the westward extension of the delta. In the Districts of Monghyr, Bhāgalpur, and the Sonthal Parganas, south of the Ganges, rock is found; and in Murshidābād District west of the Bhāgirathi, the soil is in many parts largely composed of clay and nodular limestone. And in several other parts of Bengal, where the river beds are cut in stiff clay, we find both banks high and well defined, and a greater permanence of channel.

But, ordinarily, the soil is easily acted upon, and every year, during the rainy season, large portions of land are washed away, to be reformed elsewhere by the deposition of the material thus removed. The Ganges in full flood has been known, in Rājshāhi District, to cut inland 500 feet in twelve hours, leaving deep water where solid earth was before; and, within the last twenty years, the land which was on the south bank of the Ganges, at its junction with the Brahmaputra, has come to be on the north bank, a transference of some miles of country from Faridpur District to Pabna District.

There is another way in which great changes in the courses of rivers are brought about. Owing to the extreme flatness of the country very slight differences of level determine the actual course taken, and it is often the case that a choice of courses is, so to speak, offered, and the river divides itself. Sometimes the offshoot, as the smaller branch is called, after taking for some distance an independent course, rejoins the parent stream; sometimes it strikes across country and joins another river.

It is by means of these offshoots, sometimes quite insignificant compared with the parent river, that the changes of course now to be explained are effected. It may happen, through some recent bending of the main channel above the mouth of the offshoot, or through the formation of a *char* in the main channel below the mouth of the offshoot, that the current of the main river is directed into it, with the result that an increased volume of water follows its channel, which is thereby enlarged and deepened. The stronger flow attracts more of the main river, and, gradually in the course of a few years, or violently during one rainy season, the offshoot becomes the main river. Or it may happen that in a time of exceptional floods an immense volume of water is diverted into a channel altogether incapable of controlling it. It then breaks from one channel to another, forcing its way across country until it has made for itself an entirely new course.

In this way radical changes in the river system of Bengal have been brought about. The Brahmaputra, the Tīsta, the Dāmodar have all within historical times violently broken away from their old courses, and the

The course of the Ganges from Raita to Faridpur in

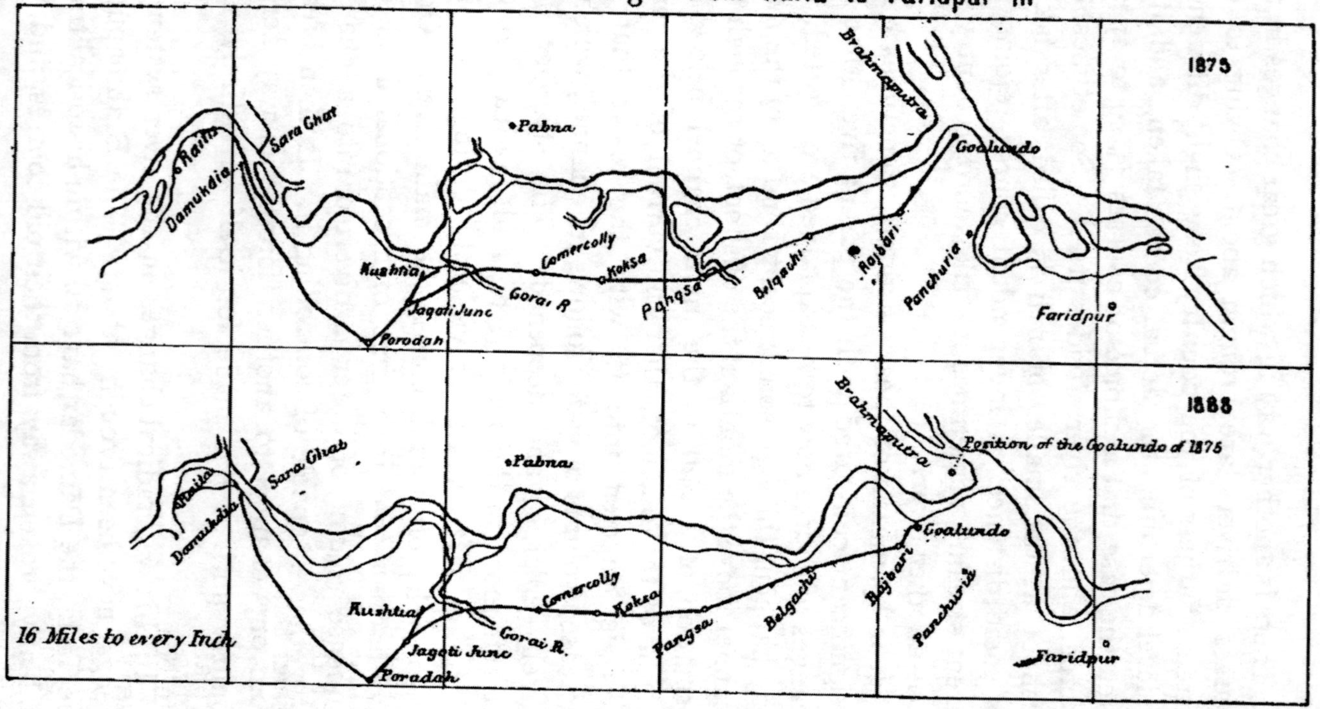

magnitude of these changes is evident from the accompanying maps. Smaller changes of a similar nature have taken place of late years. The Bāgmati, a river of north Bihār, formerly a tributary of the Buri Gandak, now joins the Tiljuga; and the Torsā, a river of northern Bengal, has deserted its former main channel, and follows that of one of its offshoots. At present the Kusi threatens a similar change of course, which may seriously affect a large part of the Purnea District.

Records of ancient capitals which once stood on the Ganges point to changes of its course which occurred in the more distant past, and give us a clue to the position of its ancient channel. Tamluk, Sātgāon, Gaur, the splendour of the last testified to by the nature and extent of the ruins which still remain, were all royal cities standing on the main river. There is strong reason to believe that the Bhāgirathi, now its most western deltaic distributary, marks the original course of the main Ganges, and that, at a time probably subsequent to the commencement of Muhammedan rule in Bengal, the river broke away to the south-east to form the present channel separating Rājshāhi and Presidency Divisions. The Brahmaputra then flowed south-east to the Meghna, and the deltas of the two rivers were doubtless much more distinct than they are now.

It is possible that volcanic action, by altering the relative levels of large areas, may have been an influence in bringing about some of the great river changes, and may also account for the continuous westerly movement of the Kusi and the Sone, which has been going on for centuries. The Sone once joined the Ganges close to Patna, and the Kusi now flows near the western border

GANGETIC RIVER SYSTEM IN THE 18th. CENTURY.

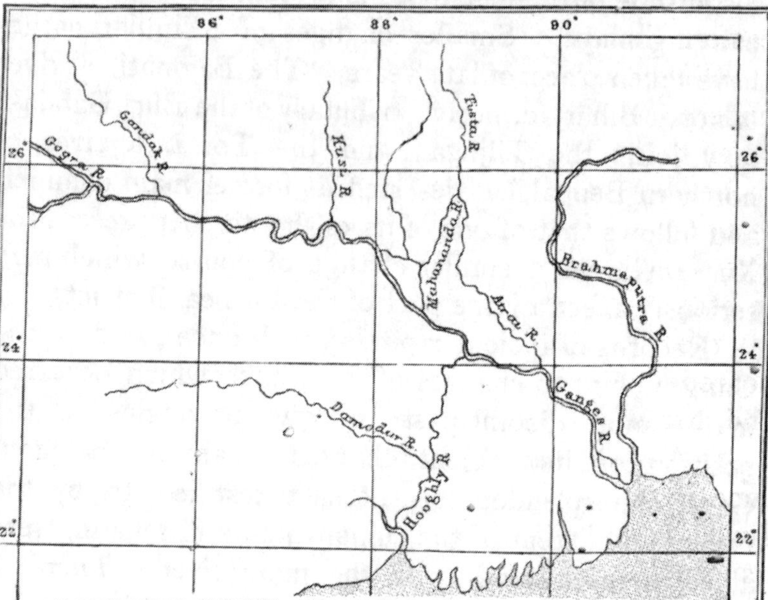

GANGETIC RIVER SYSTEM AT THE PRESENT DAY.

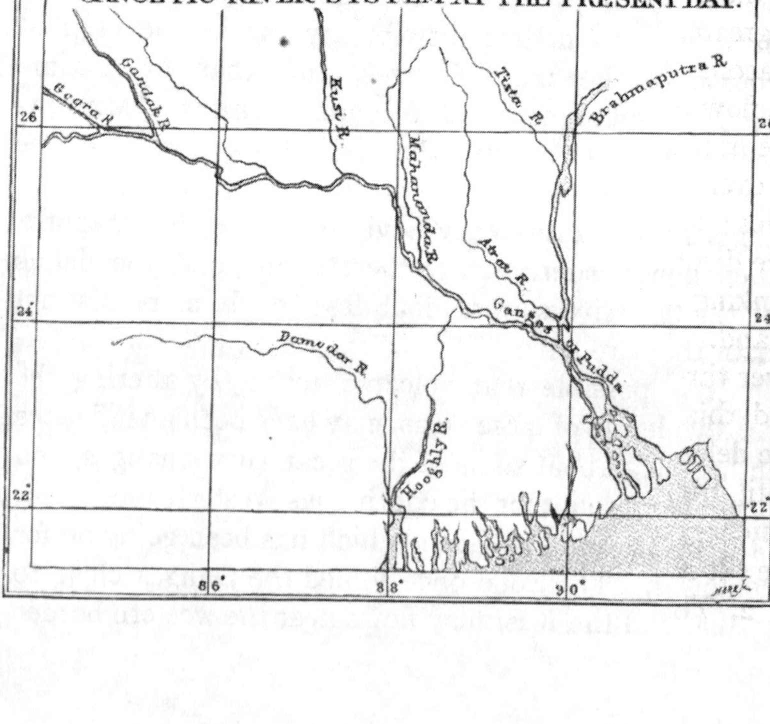

of Purnea District, whereas it once flowed on its eastern border.

We must now consider the changes which rivers undergo when they become deltaic. This happens when their average fall per mile drops to less than five inches, and the regular deposition of silt begins. The characteristic features of a delta are:—(1) The main river breaks up into distributaries; (2) the rivers flow in beds raised above the general level of the country; (3) the distributaries are unable to carry off the water poured into them when the parent river is in flood, and, hence, a delta is periodically inundated.

1. Any column of moving water will, when resistance is offered to its onward progress, tend to subdivide itself, and throw off branches right and left of its former course. This is precisely the case of a river at the commencement of its delta. It is meeting with a greater resistance to its onward course for several reasons. Owing to the greater flatness of the country its flow is less helped by gravity, and it therefore feels the friction of its bed an opposing force more difficult to overcome. There is also the influence of the sea and tides: the former acting as a constant check upon the free discharge of the river water, the latter periodically banking it up, and arresting its flow for many miles inland. Hence it is that in a delta we find the parent river throwing off distributaries, which again subdivide; and this process is repeated all the more easily that in the delta land is in its softest, least consolidated state, until, near the sea, we have a labyrinth of channels, in which current is reduced to a minimum, and most of the silt is deposited.

2. This deposition of silt begins, of course, in the

channels of the rivers, but during the rains, when the rivers overflow, and when most silt is brought down, it is deposited all over the flooded country, the level of which is thus gradually raised. The deposit is thickest near the rivers, where the flood water is muddiest, the water gradually clearing itself as it moves inland. Hence it is that the country about midway between two deltaic distributaries lies lowest, and is usually occupied by a permanent *bīl*. Here the flood water deposits the rest of its silt, and gradually drains off to a point further down the delta, where it is able to re-enter some channel and be conveyed to the sea. A section across any portion of a delta would thus have the form represented, with some exaggeration, in the diagram.

SECTION OF DELTA.

3. The beds of deltaic rivers being thus raised, the annual inundation of the delta during the rainy season is a necessary consequence. The banks of the rivers are the highest part of the country, and when once the water spills over them, as it does shortly after the commencement of the rains, the whole country goes under water. This is what happens in the truly deltaic portion of the Ganges-Brahmaputra delta. The staple crop is the long-stemmed variety of rice, which grows in water from 15 to 20 feet deep; roads are practically unknown, and the peasants go about in boats, and build their houses on the high ground bordering the rivers, or on artificial mounds.

To the oldest portions of the delta, however, this

description does not apply. As time goes on, and the level of the country is raised, the land becomes more consolidated; the *bils* silt up and get smaller; the distributaries tend to silt up, and sever their connection with the parent river; and a general inundation of the country is not the normal state of things in the rainy season. The northern, and the greater part of the western, portion of the Gangetic delta has become like this: many of the rivers are no longer distributaries in the proper sense of the word, and though they are still filled with water, they are fed by surface drainage and by percolation from the water-laden soil in which their channels are cut. Even the Hooghly and its tributaries are only kept open by constant supervision near the points where they take off from the Ganges; their currents are carefully trained in the dry season to cut away *chars*, and deepen their channels, and, notwithstanding this care, one of them, the Māthābhanga, was entirely disconnected from the Ganges during the whole of the dry season of 1894, *i.e.*, from November to June. Further evidence of the condition of this part of the delta, which comprises the greater part of Presidency Division, is found in the fact that the creeks and estuaries on the sea-face are increasingly salt towards the west.

Bordering the sea-face of the delta is the Sundarbans, a low swampy land, covered with dense jungle, and intersected in all directions by sluggish creeks. Here we have the delta in the first stage of its existence, and, as the silt-bearing river water makes its way into the sea, a struggle commences between it and the currents which work along the coast. These round off the spits of newly-formed land, and often, by depositing and piling up the sand they carry, form sand hills, which protect the land from further demolition by the sea.

Except in the east the delta of the Ganges has not materially increased within historic times, and in this respect it differs greatly from the deltas of the Po and Mississippi. This is due to a variety of causes, some of which are here mentioned. The great bulk of the silt is brought down during the four months of the rainy season, when the rivers flow very strongly, and retain much of it in suspension. Moreover most of the water is discharged by one great estuary, that of the Meghna, and recent accretions are chiefly on the islands of the estuary, and the mainland north of it. At the same time, the discharge of so large a proportion of water by an estuary is unfavourable to land making. A considerable quantity of silt is undoubtedly carried out to sea, and much is lost in an unfathomed depression known as the "Swatch of no ground," which extends for many miles near the sea-face of the western portion of the Sundarbans.

Owing to the extreme flatness of the plains most parts of them are liable to inundation from the intersecting rivers, and, at intervals, disastrous floods occur. Such floods have within the last few years swept over Sāran, Murshidābād, and Nadia Districts. Hitherto little has been done to minimise this evil beyond constructing protective embankments along the rivers.

These embankments are not an unmixed blessing. They confine to the channel of the river the fertilising silt that would otherwise have been spread abroad over the surface of the land. Another evil that sometimes follows is that the bed of the river is raised by the deposition of silt in it above the level of the neighbouring country. This has happened in the case of the Gandak in north Bihār, the Gumti in Tippera, and other rivers. When this state of things is reached the embanking has to be continued in self-defence, and every year adds to the magnitude of possible disaster in case the embankment is breached. In some instances an attempt has been made to restore a more natural state of things by cutting the embankment in some convenient place, and allowing the water to make a new course for itself. This has been done in the case of the Gumti near Comilla. The embanked river was a constant menace to the town, and the embankment has been cut through some miles below it.

The scientific embanking of rivers has been more fully carried out in the case of some European rivers. More room is allowed for flood water by constructing the main embankments at some distance from the rivers, while lower embankments protect the country within these from any but exceptional floods. In this way the deposition of silt takes place over a considerable area, and, at the same time, the ravages of flood are kept within definite bounds.

The river system of Bengal comprises several distinct systems, which will now be shortly described.

The Ganges - Brahmaputra - Meghna System.—The Ganges enters Bengal from the North-West Provinces in Pātna Division, after a course generally east from its junction with the Jumna at Allāhābād. Immediately within the boundary of the province it is joined by the *Gogra* from the north-west, a river which, unlike the Ganges, has its origin on the further side of the Himalaya in Tibet, and which, on first entering the plains, is considerably larger than the Ganges at the corresponding part of its course. Within fifty miles the Ganges is joined by two other great rivers: by the *Sone* from the south, a little west of Dinapore, and by the *Gandak* from the north-west, opposite Patna. Having received these tributaries the Ganges may be said to have reached its full size. Its course is generally east until it has passed the northern slopes of the Rājmahāl hills. Round these it sweeps to the south-east, and maintains this general direction to the sea. The Sone is the only important tributary it receives on the south bank. Other important tributaries which join it on the north bank are the *Buri Gandak* in Monghyr District, the *Kusi* in Purnea District, and the *Mahānanda* in Mālda District.

At the northern point of Presidency Division, more than 1,200 miles from its source, and 300 from the sea, the Ganges gives off its first deltaic distributary, the *Bhāgirathi*, which takes a course generally south, past Calcutta, where it is called the Hooghly, to the sea. The Bhāgirathi, before it becomes the Hooghly, receives two tributaries on its east bank, the *Jalangi* and the *Churni*, which are also offshoots from the Ganges. On the west bank it receives, as the Hooghly, two important tributaries: the *Dāmodar* and the *Rupnārāin*, which flow from the Chota Nāgpur. The Bhāgirathi, and the offshoots from the Ganges allied with it, are no longer true distributaries. Except in the rainy season the quantity of Ganges water they convey to the sea is inconsiderable. The first true distributary is the *Gorai*, or, as it is called lower down, the *Mādhumati*. This river is a fresh-water river all the year round, while those west of it, as they approach the sea, become brackish or salt.

About 40 miles east from where the Gorai branches off the Brhamaputra joins the Ganges from the north. This great river enters Bengal from Assam, and first touches the Province on the eastern border of Rangpur District. Its course to the Ganges is generally south. Within the Province it receives several tributaries, all on the right or west bank. The chief are the *Rāydak*, *Dharlla*, and *Tīsta* in Rangpur District, and the combined *Karatoa* and *Atrāi* in Pabna District. On its east bank it sends off distributaries.. The first of these is in many respects the analogue of the Bhāgirathi. It marks the ancient channel of the main river, which until the beginning of this century flowed across Mymensingh District to the Meghna, and it is locally still called the Brahmaputra. Also, like the Bhāgirathi, it is ceasing to be a true distributary, and, except in the rains, carries off but little water from the parent river. The chief real distributary of the Brahmaputra is the *Dhaleswari* river, which flows through Dācca District to the Meghna.

After the union of the Ganges and Brahmaputra the chief offshoot is the *Ariāl Khān*, which leaves the main river in Faridpur District, and distributes its water over the Bāckergunge Sundarbans. The *Padda*, as the combined Ganges and Brahmaputra is locally called, is joined, at the south-east corner of Dācca District, by the Meghna bringing down the drainage of South Assam; and the great river thus formed is thenceforth called the Meghna, and enters the Bay of Bengal by a broad estuary 80 miles in length, studded with low silt-formed islands. The rivers of Tippera and Noākhāli Districts flow into the Meghna or its estuary.

The Ganges and Brahmaputra are wide and deep rivers throughout their courses in Bengal, navigable at all times by river steamers, and native crafts of the largest size. Islands and side channels are common, especially in the Brahmaputra. At its lowest the Ganges varies from 400 yards to 1¼ miles in width, and its depth is about 30 feet. In the rains, the rise is very great, lessening, of course, towards the delta and the sea. The average rise in the Ganges and Brahmaputra is about 30 feet. The following were the actual heights above the dry season level on the 28th of August, 1894, at various points on the Ganges: Buxār, 28½ feet; Monghyr, 27 feet; Sāhibgang, 26 feet; Goalando, at the junction of the Ganges and Brahmaputra, 21 feet. At this time of the year these rivers fill their whole channels, and in many parts overflow, and flood the country for miles along their banks; while, by blocking the mouths of their tributaries, they often cause them also to overflow.

2. *The Chittagong Rivers.*—These rivers, of which the chief are the *Karnaphuli*, *Sangu*, and *Mātāmuri*, drain the ranges of the Hill Tracts, and, on leaving the hills, flow, more or less at right angles to their former courses, across the strip of alluvial plain to the sea.

3. *The Orissa Rivers.*—These rivers drain the hill country of the central provinces, Chota Nāgpur and Orissa, and enter the Bay of Bengal after a short course across the plains of Orissa. They have two characteristics common to all rivers draining the highlands of central India, namely, the extreme difference between their volume in the dry season and the rainy season, and the rapidity with which they rise into flood after rain. These characteristics are ex-

plained by the nature of their origin and course. None of them are snow-fed, and the rainfall of the country they drain is smaller, and, at the same time, distributed over fewer months of the year than the rainfall of a great part of the country drained by the Gangetic system. Moreover, as their drainage area is of much less extent, and, for the most part, hilly, the flow of the rivers is rapid. The consequence is that in the dry months these rivers run very low and some become insignificant, especially in their upper courses. When rain falls it usually falls over the whole of their drainage area, and is at once discharged by small mountain feeders into the main streams, which rise with great suddenness. The Mahānadi has an average dry season discharge, at the point where it enters the plains not 70 miles from the sea, of 3,000 cubic feet per second, which is less than that of the Ganges at Hardwār, a thousand miles from the sea. On the other hand the maximum flood discharge of the Mahānadi is 1,800,000 cubic feet per second, which is equal to that of the Ganges at its greatest; a volume far beyond the capacity of its deltaic distributaries to carry off. Hence the liability of the Mahānadi delta to excessive floods.

The most northern of the Orissa rivers in the *Subarnarekha*, which rises in the Rānchi tableland of Chota Nāgpur, and enters the sea in Balasore district. The *Bāitarani* rises in the Orissa Native State of Keonjhar, and, after a circuitous course among the hills, enters the plains on the borders of Cuttack and Balasore. The *Brāhmani* is formed by the union of the South Koil and Sankh rivers of Chota Nāgpur, and flows for the greatest part of its course through the hill country of the Native States of Chota Nāgpur and

Orissa. The *Mahānadi* rises in the central provinces, and flows for the most part in them. It enters the Orissa plains through the Narāj Gorge, seven miles above Cuttack. These three rivers, the Bāitarani, Brāhmani, and Mahānadi, in their course through the plains, practically form one great delta. They are all inter-connected by means of the distributaries into which they break up on leaving the hills. The bulk of the water of the Bāitarani and Brāhmani rivers finds its way into the sea by the Dhāmra estuary; that of the Mahānadi chiefly at False Point.

CLIMATE.

Although Bengal is only partly within the tropics, its climate is essentially tropical. The year is divided into three well-marked seasons: the cold, the hot, and the rainy; the relative character and extent of which vary in different parts of the province. As we proceed inland from the coast towards the North-West Provinces, the cold season is colder and longer, the hot season hotter, the rains begin later and end sooner, and the climate altogether is drier than it is further east. Speaking generally, the cold season may be said to extend from November to March, the hot season from March to June, and the rainy season from the middle of June to October. The cold season is least marked in Orissa. In the wetter northern and eastern districts a considerable proportion of the total rainfall (about one-eighth) comes down in the three months preceding the rainy season, and in these parts the hot weather is not so severe.

The climate of Bengal is regarded as being exceptionally humid, and the actual quantity of water-vapour present in the air, even in the driest parts, is always considerably greater than in London. But if we take the more usual way of measuring dampness, and compare the actual quantity of vapour in the air with that which would be necessary to saturate it, we find the official returns showing that the percentage of saturation of London air is greater than that of Calcutta air in every month of the year except June, July, and August. And as it is the percentage of saturation which indicates the readiness of air to part with its moisture and make things damp, the figures would seem to show that the popular opinion of the dampness of the Bengal climate is only partially true. The average percentage of saturation for the year in Calcutta is 77; in Patna 65, and in London, 89. But it must be remembered that these figures for Bengal are based on observations taken during the day, and that temperature in Bengal is subject to much greater and more sudden changes than in England, especially in the cold season. A fall of temperature rapidly raises the degree of saturation, and the air of Bengal is undoubtedly very much damper after sunset, and before the sun is well up, than during the day. The cold-weather fogs so common in Bengal in the early morning are visible proof that the air is more than saturated with water-vapour, and observations taken in the early morning would undoubtedly yield much higher figures for humidity than those taken when the air has become heated by the sun.

The driest month in Bengal is April, but all the earlier months of the year are comparatively dry, and it is this dryness, by promoting evaporation from the skin, that makes the excessive heat of the hot season bearable. Fortunately, too, the dryness increases as we go up country, where the temperatures rise higher.

The mean annual temperature varies from 80° in Cuttack District to 74° in Chota Nāgpur, the lower average in the latter case being partly due to the elevation (about 2,000 feet) of most of the observing stations. The mean annual temperature of Calcutta is 78°, of Patna 77°, and of Chittagong 76°, The highest temperature ever registered in the shade in Calcutta was 107·7°, and the lowest 45°. But the table at the end of this section, which states the *average* maximum and minimum temperatures, for the hottest and coldest months of the year, for each Division, gives a better idea of the climate, so far as it depends upon temperature, than such special figures.

During the cold weather the prevailing winds are northerly. In February, as the temperature begins to rise, winds set in from the sea, and, by degrees, penetrate further and further inland. In the western part of the Province hot dry winds, which have blown across from the west of India, prevail during the hot months, and it is not until the break of the rains in June that the real south-west monsoon sets in. Storms of short duration occur occasionally during the hot season, and temporarily cool the air. The more serious storms, known as cyclones, are formed in the Bay, expend their fury there and on the seaboard districts, and break up rapidly as they proceed inland. They happen most frequently in the months of May, October, and November, less often in June and December, but they have been known to occur in every month of the year except February. Storms of similar character but of less intensity are common in the rainy season. They differ, however, from the more violent cyclones in the great distance they can travel. They are not broken up by hills of more than a thousand feet high, and have been known to travel across India for more than a thousand miles.

Name of Division.	Average Maximum Temperatures.		Average Minimum Temperatures.		Mean Annual Rainfall.
	January.	May.	January.	May.	
Patna	72·7	100·5	50·4	77	44·5
Bhāgalpur	75·2	96·3	49·9	75·5	54·5
Burdwān	79·0	99·4	54·8	77·5	57·6
Presidency	77·2	94·5	55·0	77·2	60·4
Rājshāhi, (Darjeeling being omitted)	74·9	90·6	50·3	73·3	86·9
Dācca	75·8	90·3	53·8	75·1	78·3
Chittagong	77·7	88·8	53·7	75·2	103
Chota Nāgpur	75·6	99·9	51·4	75·6	52·2
Orissa	81·2	96·0	58·6	78·8	58·5

The rainfall of Bengal varies between 42 inches per annum in Shāhābād District, and 212·25 inches at Baxa on the Bhutān frontier in Jalpāiguri District. The average annual rainfall in Calcutta is 63·44 inches. In the south-east of England the annual rainfall is only 24 inches, but this is distributed much more uniformly over the year than the rainfall of Bengal, of which by far the greatest part comes down during the rainy season. At this time of year very large falls often take place within 24 hours. The largest ever registered was 35 inches, but this of course is most exceptional. But falls of several inches are common. The regions of heaviest rainfall are the districts along the coast, which are first struck by the monsoon current, and the hill districts of the north and east, together with the plains bordering them.

Plants and Animals.

The usual aspect of the plains is tame: a monotonous expanse of cultivated land, here and there broken, where the villages are, by plantations of bamboos, date palms, plantains, and other trees recommended by their utility. The roads are sometimes bordered by trees, and in parts of Bihār mango groves are common, and give the country a picturesqueness which it elsewhere lacks. Of the arable land of the Province 57 per cent. is estimated to be under rice. The rice crop may be divided into three main classes. 1. *Aus*, or early rice is sown, with the first showers of April or May, on land which is not inundated during the rains. It is harvested in July, August, and September and is a cheap, coarse rice. 2. *Aman*, or winter rice. This kind is by far the most extensively cultivated, and includes the finer and more valuable varieties. It is sown in nurseries in April or May, transplanted from June to August, growing well in knee-deep water, and is reaped in November or December. A coarser variety grows in marshes. Its growth keeps pace with the gradual rise of the water, and its stems attain a length of from 10 to 20 feet. 3. *Boro*, or spring rice, is also a coarser and less nutritious variety. It is cultivated on *chars*, edges of *bīls*, and soft, marshy lands. It is sown in October or November, transplanted in December, and harvested in April, May, or June.

Other food crops are :—*Cereals :* various millets and pulses, wheat, barley, and maize. *Vegetables :* the egg-plant (brinjal), coomra (a climbing gourd), garlic, cabbage, spinach, radishes, onions, potatoes. *Condiments :* turmeric, ginger, chillies, coriander, and aniseed. *Fruits :* plantain, mango, pineapple, jack-fruit, guava, custard-apple, lichee, and varieties of fig and melon. Cocoa nuts are common in Eastern Bengal, but will not grow far inland.

Other important crops are *sugar-cane* and *indigo, pān* or betel leaf (a creeper), *betel* or areca nut, *Indian hemp* (grown for the intoxicating drug, *ganja,* prepared from it), the *opium poppy, tobacco, tea, cinchona. Fibre plants* are jute and cotton. *Oil seeds* are linseed, mustard, rape, sesamum. An oil is expressed from the kernel of cocoa nuts, and the the fibre is made into coir.

As we approach the hills cultivation diminishes, and the country becomes jungly. The term jungle does not merely apply to forest ; any wild, uncultivated land is called jungle, whether covered with low scrub and grass, or timber, or high grass capable of concealing an elephant. The hills of the Province are generally densely wooded to the summits, and there is often an undergrowth of grass and thorny shrubs which is almost impenetrable. In the plains immense tracts of tree and high grass jungle occupy the country at the foot of the Himalaya in Darjeeling and Jalpāiguri districts, and the western portion of the Sundarbans is also dense forest. But patches of jungle are found all over Bengal. The great jungles are mostly Government forests, and are protected and made a source of revenue.

The most valuable timber trees are the *sāl*. found all over the province, a heavy, durable wood, largely used for railway sleepers; *sīsu*, a good furniture wood; *tun*, a light, red wood, common in the Darjeeling forests; *sundri*, the commonest tree in the Sundarbans, used for boat-building, and largely brought into Calcutta for firewood. The bamboo is universal, and is put to a great variety of uses. Other trees valued for shade or ornament are the *banyan*, *pipal* or sacred fig, *mango*, *nīm*, *almond*, *tamarind*, *casuarina*, *poinciana regia* (gold mohur tree), the scarlet-flowered cotton tree (*Bombax*), the oak-like *mahua*, whose dried flower is an important article of food in parts of South Bihār, and many more. In the Himalaya the *oak*, *chestnut*, *magnolia*, *pine* and *rhododendron* flourish. Sir Joseph Hooker speaks of "vegetation of every hue, glossy-green *Garciniæ* and figs, broad plantains, feathery *Cassia* and acacias, dark *Mesua*, red-purple *Terminalia*, leafless scarlet-flowered *Bombax*, and grey *Casuarina*."

The domestic animals are the same as those of England, with the addition of the elephant and buffalo. Among wild animals are the *wild elephant*, *wild ox*, *rhinoceros*, *buffalo*, *tiger*, *bear*, *leopard*, *wild hog*, *civet cat*, *jackal*, *deer* and *monkeys* of various kinds.

Reptiles are the long-snouted fish-eating crocodile or *gavial*, and the blunt-nosed man-eating crocodile or *mugger*. Venomous snakes are common: the chief are the *cobra*, *daboia* or Russell's viper, and the *karait*.

The rivers abound in fish; the best are the *bhetki*, *hilsa*, *rui*, and *tapsi* or mango fish.

Birds are numerous, except in Sikkim; but few of them have agreeable notes, though their plumage is often gorgeous. The cuckoo is heard in the Darjeeling hills. The ordinary game birds: snipe, wild duck, teal, &c., are common.

POPULATION.*

According to the census of February, 1891, the population of Bengal was 74,643,366, the net increase since the census of 1881 being estimated at about 6 per cent. This represents an average density of population of 398 persons per square mile, while the average for England and Wales is 497. But the population of England is largely concentrated in the great towns, while that of Bengal is mainly rural. The total urban population of Bengal is under four millions; only eight towns besides Calcutta had, in 1891, over 50,000 inhabitants. These were, in order of size, Patna (165,192), Howrah (116,606), Dācca (82,321), Gāya (80,383), Darbhanga (73,561), Bhāgalpur (69,106), Chapra (57,352), Monghyr (57,077). In 1891, there were in England and Wales 62 towns with more than 50,000 inhabitants. The most thickly populated part of the Province is Bihār, with 596 persons to the square mile; Bengal Proper comes next with 510 to the square mile; Orissa and Chota Nāgpur have 233 and 150 respectively. The most densely-populated district is Sāran, with a population density of 930; the Chittagong Hill Tracts are least densely populated, with only twenty persons to the square mile.

Of the total population in 1891, 47,821,468 were Hindus; 23,658,347 were Musalmāns; 2,753,061 professed Animistic religions—the faiths of the so-

* The population of the Province, as here given, does not include that of Sikkim, South Lushāi, or the British subjects in the French settlement of Chandernagore.

called aboriginal tribes of Chota Nāgpur and elsewhere. The rest of the population was divided among Christians, Buddhists, and other smaller sects. The number of Europeans by birth was 10,856, and the total number of pure Europeans, whether by birth or descent, 22,773. Eurasians numbered 15,162.

Except in Presidency, Rājshāhi, Dācca, and Chittagong Divisions, the Hindus greatly outnumber the Musalmāns Their numbers are about equal in Presidency Division; and in Rājshāhi, Dācca and Chittagong Divisions, the Musalmāns outnumber the Hindus by about two to one. Only three millions of the population can read and write, and of these the proportion of Hindus to their total numbers is twice as great as in the case of Musalmāns. Excluding students, the number able to read and write English is under 150,000. Bengāli is the mother-tongue of more than half the population, and Hindī of more than one-third. Uriya is spoken by 95 per cent. of the inhabitants of Orissa, being the mother-tongue of nearly six millions of people, and about three millions speak one or other of the minor languages.

Nearly 48 millions of the population are engaged in agriculture and kindred pursuits. The great majority of the peasant class cultivate small holdings, in which they have a right of tenancy that can be sold or handed on from father to son. The number of landless day labourers is comparatively small.

The birth-rate of Bengal is estimated to be 48 per thousand inhabitants per annum; the death-rate 40. The figures for England and Wales are about 30·5 and 19 respectively. It thus appears that the population of Bengal renews itself oftener than that of England;

that the generations pass more quickly away. Climate, no doubt, has much to do with this; men wear out sooner in the tropics; but other conditions affecting logevity have to be taken into consideration, such as the sanitary surroundings of the people, and the abudance or lack of food. Impure drinking water and inadequate subsoil drainage have much to do with the fearful ravages of cholera and fever, and the ill-nourished systems of too large a proportion of the poorer classes invite attack, and unfit them to resist disease. It is true to say that no year passes without at least a threatening of famine in some part of the Province.

The material condition of the people is by far the best in Northern and Eastern Bengal, and in many of the districts of this part the peasantry may be called prosperous. The land is less densely populated, and wages are consequently higher and food cheaper; also some of the staple crops, such as jute and tobacco, command a higher price relative to the rent of the land than the crops of other parts. In Bihār poverty is the rule; rice is too dear to be the principal food, and its place is largly taken by cheaper grains, such as maize, the millets, barley, and peas.

PRODUCTS, INDUSTRIES, COMMERCE.

The chief vegetable products have already been enumerated.

The most important mineral product of Bengal is coal, the total output of which in 1892 exceeded 1,700,000 tons, less than one-tenth of the output of the United Kingdom in the same year.

The chief coal fields occur in the north-eastern

border of Chota Nāgpur, and in the north-west corner of Burdwān Division; but coal is worked in other parts of these Divisions, and has been found in the Darjeeling Hills. The coal is inferior to English, containing more ash and less carbon; but the strikes in England have given a great impulse to this industry, and steamers trading in the East have now adapted their furnaces to Indian coal, and use it instead of English.

Iron ore is found in various parts of the Province, and has always been more or less worked. It is now smelted on a large scale by an English Company from the ores (chiefly clay iron-stone) found in the neighbourhood of the Burdwān coal field. Copper is found and fitfully worked in Darjeeling District and Sikkim, and also in Chota Nāgpur. Gold is also found in Chota Nāgpur, but whether in sufficient quantity to be profitably worked yet remains to be seen. Mica is found in Chota Nāgpur, and in the hills on the south border of Patna Division, and in Bhāgalpur.

The preparation of products for use or export gives rise to some important industries. The chief of these are the manufactures of *jute*, *opium*, *tea*, *indigo*, *silk*, *tobacco*, *sugar*, *saltpetre*, *salt*, and *lac*. Jute and tea are the most important; indigo and silk are declining industries. Opium is a very valuable Government monopoly. Jute is either exported as fibre, or woven into a coarse cloth used for packing, and for making gunny bags in which other produce is exported. Lac dye is in less demand than formerly, owing to the competition of aniline dyes, but the resinous portion of the stick-lac, which is a deep orange-coloured incrustation found on the branches of various trees in the jungles of Chota Nāgpur and Western Burdwān, is largely manufactured into shellac. Saltpetre is extracted from the saliferous soil which abounds in parts of Patna and Bhāgalpur Divisions. Salt is manufactured by evaporation in the salt tracts of the Orissa Coast.

Unlike England, which does not produce enough grain to feed its population, Bengal does not require to import food stuffs, and, indeed, is a large exporter of rice and wheat. The following list gives the chief exports arranged in order of the values exported in 1893-4: *Raw jute, tea, opium, oil-seeds, manufactured jute, rice, indigo, hides* and *skins, lac, raw cotton, raw silk, wheat.* On the other hand, Bengal cannot compete with Lancashire in the manufacture of cotton, and cotton goods are the chief articles of import. The other chief imports arranged in order of the values imported during 1893-4 are *metals, mineral oil, machinery, woollen goods, salt, liquors, sugar, hardware.*

INTERNAL COMMUNICATIONS.

At the beginning of 1894 there were about 2,670 miles of railway, and 673 miles of navigable canal in Bengal. In the United Kingdom, over an area less by about one-third, there were at the end of 1892, 20,325 miles of railway and 3,813 miles of canal. Bengal, however, has in the Ganges and Brahmaputra, and their numerous tributaries, a magnificent natural system of internal communications, to which the railways and canals must be regarded as supplementary; so that the disproportion between the two countries as regards facilities for internal communication is not so great as would at first sight appear. The main streams of the Ganges and Brahmaputra are navigable by inland steamers, and are connected with the Hooghly and

Calcutta by boat and steamer routes across the Delta; their tributaries in North Bihār are navigable by country boats of greater or less burthen to the Nepāl frontier, and their other tributaries in Northern and Eastern Bengal are similarly navigable for the greater part of their courses. The rivers of South Bihār, Western Bengal, Chota Nāgpur, and the Orissa Native States are, owing to their great variations of volume, less convenient for navigation, but all are to some extent utilised. The Orissa rivers also are navigable in their course through the plains. There are, besides, over 4,000 miles of metalled roads, and over 31,000 miles of unmetalled roads: the Burdwān Division having the greatest mileage of metalled road, and Patna Division the greatest mileage of unmetalled road. Faridpur District has least road communication, but in this District, as in several others, the rivers are the ordinary highways.

Orissa and Chota Nāgpur, isolated as they always have been from the rest of Bengal by defective communications, are also the worst off in the means of internal communication. In the case of Chota Nāgpur, a hilly and jungly country, mainly inhabited by aboriginal tribes of backward civilization, this defect has not been so much felt; but Orissa has suffered much through its isolation. It has now an extensive system of canals to supplement and connect its river communications, and is also connected by canal with Western Bengal and the Hooghly. Not the least of the services rendered by the railways and canals is that they have made it possible to relieve scarcity and avert famine by speedily throwing supplies of food from one part of the Province to another.

The railways of Bengal are chiefly of two gauges: the broad gauge and the metre gauge. The East Indian Railway, which has its terminus at Howrah, opposite Calcutta, and connects Bengal with the North-West Provinces, the Central Provinces, and Bombay, is a broad-gauge system, serving Bengal west of the delta, and the right bank of the Ganges. The Bengal-Nāgpur Railway, which provides an alternative route across India, branches off from it at Assansol in Burdwān District. The Eastern Bengal Railway, also broad gauge, serves the delta, and is connected with the East Indian Railway by a bridge across the Hooghly about 23 miles above Calcutta. North of the Ganges is a metre-gauge system, composed of a number of lines running from the river north or north-west towards the Himalaya. These are connected by cross branches, and the whole system, in which through running is only broken by the river Kusi, is joined to a metre-gauge system in the North-West Provinces, which serves the country north of the Gogra. There are several subsidiary lines of smaller gauge, one of which connects the Northern Bengal system with the Brahmaputra. This river, and the rivers and railways of North Bihār and North Bengal bring down produce to the Ganges. It is then conveyed to Calcutta by boat or steamer, or transhipped to the East Indian Railway on the south bank, or in the delta, to the Eastern Bengal Railway. In these ways the produce of the Province is collected in Calcutta for export, and the imports are in like manner distributed. The trade returns of the last few years show that the inland water-borne trade of Calcutta is something less than half the rail-borne trade; but, taking into consideration the slowness of water transit, and that the shortest channels leading up country from the Hooghly are only really open during the rainy season, we can realize the great extent of the water traffic that goes on.

PART II.

GEOGRAPHY OF THE DIVISIONS.

As we have seen, the Province of Bengal is divided into four sub-provinces, in each of which the territory under direct British administration is divided into Divisions. These nine Divisions will now be separately described. The Native States will be treated of under the Division with which they are politically and naturally associated, except in the case of the Orissa and Chota Nāgpur Native States, which will be described under the sub-provinces to which they belong.

The Divisions will be taken in the order of the list given in Part I.

BENGAL PROPER.

Area: 70,532 square miles. Population: 38,277,339.

I. PRESIDENCY DIVISION:

Area: 12,066 square miles. Population: 8,535,126.

Districts.	*Area.*	*Population.*
Calcutta	20 ...	681,560
24-Parganas	2,108 ...	1,892,033
Nadia	2,793 ...	1,644,108
Murshidābād	2,143 ...	1,250,946
Jessore	2,925 ...	1,888,827
Khulna	2,077 ...	1,177,652

Name, Boundaries, &c.—The Presidency of Fort William in Bengal was constituted in 1707, and the

PRESIDENCY DIVISION

Scale 1 Inch=48 Miles.

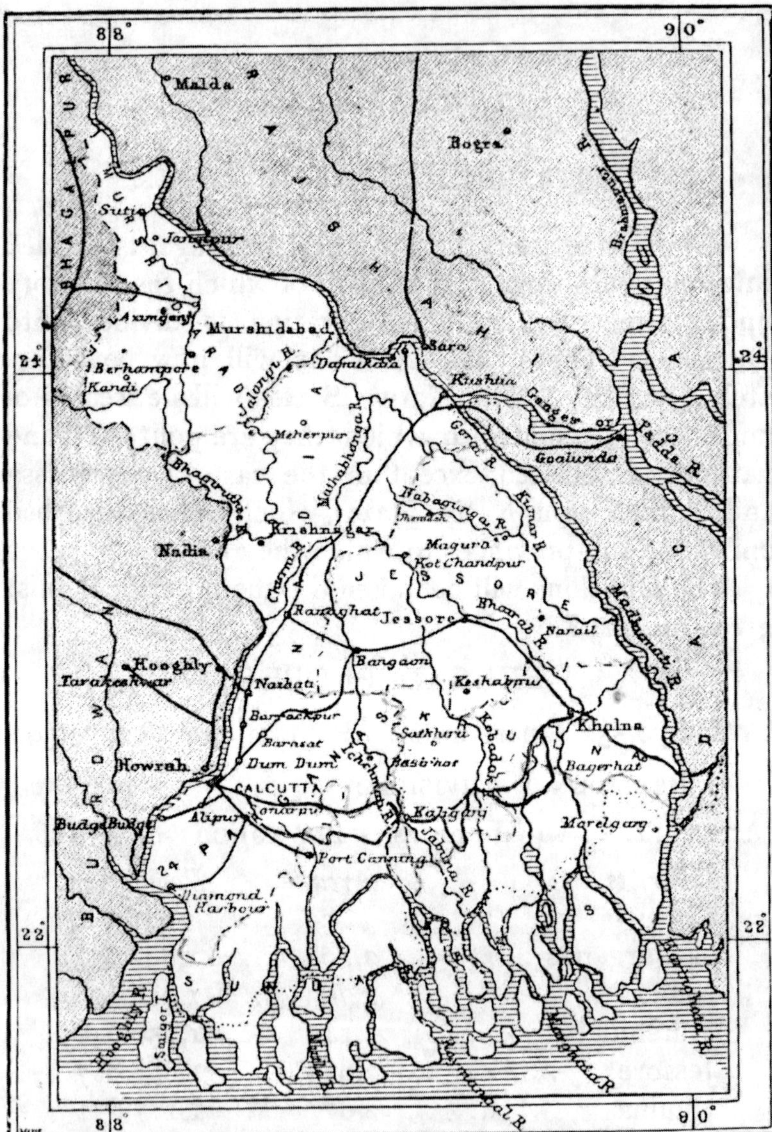

Divisional Boundary ------------ Canal ____________

District Boundary -.-.-.-.-.-.- Steamer Routes ....

modern Division, which includes the original "Presidency," takes its name accordingly. The Division may be described as triangular in shape, with its vertex to the north projecting into Bhāgalpur Division. It is separated from Rājshāhi Division in the north-east by the Ganges or Padda; from Dācca Division on the east by the Madhumāti; from Burdwān Division on the west by the Bhāgirathi and its continuation the Hooghly, from a point near Plassey in the north of Nadia District. On the south lie the Sundarbans and the sea.

For administrative purposes the Division is divided into six Districts: Murshidābād in the north; south of this, Nadia; the 24-Parganas in the south-west; Khulna in the south-east; and Jessore in the east, between Nadia and Khulna. Calcutta and its suburbs, though geographically within the 24-Parganas, rank as a separate District.

Size and Population.—The length of the Division is about 220 miles, and its greatest breadth about 120 miles. Its area is 12,066 square miles, which is almost equal to that of the six northern counties of England, the East Riding of Yorkshire being omitted. The populations of these two areas are also nearly the same; the population of Presidency Division being 8,535,126, and that of the six northern counties, less the East Riding, 8,648,278. As might be expected from the nature of the country, the population of Presidency Division is more uniformly distributed than that of the six northern counties; it varies from a maximum density of 897 to the square mile in the 24-Parganas, to a minimum of 566 in Khulna; while Lancashire has a population density of 2,080, and Westmoreland, the most thinly populated country, only 84 to the square mile.

Physical Features.—With the exception of the part of Murshidābād District west of the Bhāgirathi, Presidency Division forms the western portion of the Gangetic delta. It is a vast alluvial plain, minutely intersected by rivers, which, as in all deltas, mark the highest level of the country through which they flow. The low levels between the rivers collect the surface drainage and form *bils*. The highest point in the delta is in Murshidābād, where the elevation reaches 64 feet above the level of the sea. From this, southwards, there is a gradual descent to 55 feet in Nadia, and 19 feet in Jessore. Calcutta is 18 feet above mean sea level, and, further south, we sink to the Sundarbans, which are barely above the level of the sea.

Most of that portion of the delta comprised in Presidency Division has the characteristics of a delta at a late period of its existence. Its rivers no longer carry to the sea any large proportion of the water of the Ganges, and their connections with the parent river continually tend to silt up. It is only by constant care that the headwaters of the Bhāgirathi, Jalangi, and Māthābhanga can be kept open for navigation, and were it not for the scouring of their channels by the immense volumes of water that are poured into them from the Ganges in the rainy season, they would soon lose their connection with it. However, notwithstanding the fact that these rivers receive, during the dry season of the year, comparatively little water from the parent river, they fill themselves by percolation from the sodden country they traverse, and, even if they lost all connection with the Ganges, they would still remain considerable rivers in the lower parts of their courses.

In the northern part of the Division the river system is simple, but as we approach the Sundarbans the network of streams becomes so intricate that a systematic description is scarcely possible. The rivers constantly change their names, and the offshoots are so numerous that it is often hard to say which is to be regarded as the main channel.

The head of the delta is near Suti in Murshidābād District. Here the *Bhāgirathi*, the first deltaic distributary, branches off from the Ganges. In April, 1894, the depth of water at the entrance from the Ganges was only 3 feet 6 inches. In the middle of August, at the height of the rains, it was 22 feet. The course of the river from Suti is south through Murshidābād District, which it divides into two portions, differing remarkably from each other in natural features. The country to the west is mainly a stiff clay, often terminating in cliffs overhanging the river. This soil is little acted on by water, and practically fixes the western limit of the delta. East of the river the country is ordinary alluvial plain, and the frequent changes in the course of the river are due to the ease with which it is acted upon. The battle-field of Plassey has thus been entirely washed away, and, lower down the river, the town of Nadia, formerly on the east bank, is now, owing to a change of course, on the west bank, and separated by the river from the District of which it is the ancient capital. The case of Cossimbuzar has already been referred to (p. 13). The banks of the Bhāgirathi are lined by artificial embankments to prevent the flooding of the country during the rains.

Occasionally, when the rise of the river is exceptionally high, the embankments are breached, and disastrous floods occur. The flood water makes its way south-east, through the low-lying interior of Murshidābād District, to the Jalangi, and onwards to the Māthābhanga, and has several times of late years caused serious breaks in the railway which crosses Nadia District south of the last-named river.

Near the town of Nadia the Bhāgirathi is joined by the *Jalangi* which takes off from the Ganges at the boundary of Murshidābād and Nadia Districts, and is the boundary between them for about fifty miles. Its course is very tortuous, but at the present time it is the most navigable of the rivers which connect the Hooghly with the Ganges in the north of the Division, and is the route taken during the rainy season by steamers making for the Ganges on their way up-country, or to Assam. In April, 1894, at the entrance from the Ganges, there were six feet of water; in the middle of August twenty-three feet.

The next offshoot from the Ganges is the Māthābhanga, which takes off about ten miles below the Jalangi. The Māthābanga throws off a branch called the *Kumār*, a feeder of the Madhumāti, and, further on, the *Ichchamati*. Both these rivers flow to the Sundarbans. After throwing off the latter the Māthābhanga is called the *Churni*, and joins the Hooghly a little below Sāntipur. It is from a little above this town that the Bhāgirathi is called the Hooghly. During the early part of the century the Māthābhanga was the most navigable of these rivers, but at present its entrance from the Ganges is absolutely closed during the dry season, and had only eight feet of water in the rainy season of 1894.

After receiving the Churni the Hooghly receives no other tributaries of importance from within the

THE HOOGHLY, AT CALCUTTA (ABOVE HOWRAH BRIDGE), SHOWING NATIVE SHIPPING.

division. It has a course from this point of about 120 miles to the sea, becoming near Calcutta a broad tidal river. Ships drawing 26 feet come up to Calcutta, but, owing to the continual shifting of the deep-water channel, and the peculiarly treacherous nature of the sandbanks, its navigation is very dangerous.

The main stream of the Ganges, though it nowhere enters the division, forms its north-east boundary for about 150 miles, its channel varying in width from a mile to four miles. In the dry season the current flows at the rate of about three miles an hour, and its average depth is about 30 feet. During the rains the river more than doubles its rate of flow, and adds between 20 and 30 feet to its depth. At this season it acts violently upon its banks, and it is doubtful if any part of it occupies the same channel that it did 20 years ago. None of the railway termini on the river have anything but temporary stations. Several attempts have been made to make permanent stations, but these have all, sooner or later, been destroyed by the river.

The other rivers of the division are those which make their way into the sea through the Sundarbans. The Kumār and Ichchamati, offshoots from the Māthābhangha, have already been mentioned. The latter of these is known lower down as the *Jabuna*, and near the sea as the *Rāymangal*. Between this river and the Hooghly there is no big river which flows from the north of the division, but, east of Calcutta, the *Bidyādhari* flows with curiously circuitous course and many interlacings to the Matla at Port Canning. This river is connected with the Hooghly at Calcutta by two canals—Tolly's nullah and the Bāliāghāta canal—and forms part of the boat route from Calcutta across the Sundarbans. The *Matla* is a fine river, navigable by sea-going ships, and has a course of about 60 miles through the Sundarbans to the sea.

From the Matla boats pass by various channels to the Ichchamati-Jabuna, and thence by a cross channel to the *Kobādak*, which is the next big river to the east. This river is a good example of the changes taking place in this part of the delta. Half a century ago it was an offshoot from the Māthābhangha before its bifurcation into the Churni and Ichchamati. Now the connection between the two has entirely silted up, and the Kobadak in its upper course is a much smaller river than it used to be. Lower down it fills itself by percolation, and is a large river. For some distance it forms the boundary between the 24-Parganas and Khulna District, and its main branch eventually enters the sea as the *Pangæ*.

In the upper part of its course the Kobadak throws off the *Bhāirāb*, which flows through Jessore and Khulna. The Bhāirāb has suffered through the deterioration of the upper Kobadak, and is now insignificant at Jessore, but near Khulna it has recovered itself, and one of its branches reaches the sea as the *Marghāta*. A little east of Khulna the other branch receives the *Athārabanka* from the Mādhumati, and this is the channel taken by boats crossing from the Hooghly.

This branch of the Bhāirāb, which retains the name, flows into the Mādhumati lower down. The *Mādhumati* is the first true deltaic distributary we meet in proceeding east from the Hooghly. It is formed by the union of the *Kumār*, the *Noboganga*, and the *Gorai*, which last leaves the Ganges at Kushtia, about 35 miles below the outlet of the

Māthābhanga. The Mādhumati is navigable by inland steamers all the year round, and is a fresh-water stream to the sea; while the rivers west of it are increasingly salt to the Hooghly. It has a course of about 100 miles, and forms most of the eastern boundary of the division. In the lower part of its course it is called the *Baleswar*, and its estuary the *Haringhāta*. All the rivers of the division are affected by the tide to a point about 100 miles from the sea.

The whole of Presidency Division is liable to flood during the rainy season. In the northern and better raised parts such floods are a calamity; and the rivers are bordered by protective embankments which make a general flooding of the country only an occasional occurrence. As we go south we find it more and more normal for the country to be under water in the rains, and the soil receives a top-dressing of silt deposited by the flood water which constantly renews its fertility. In these parts the embankments are rather intended to regulate and control the floods than prevent them, while the lower lying fields towards the sea are embanked in order to keep out the salt water.

Between Presidency Division proper and the sea is the Sundarbans, a labyrinth of creeks and rivers buried in jungle, and uninhabited except by tigers and other wild animals. This unsurveyed tract occupies the sea face of the delta, extending from Saugor Island, at the mouth of the Hooghly, to the Meghna, a distance of about 165 miles. Its area is estimated at 5,309 square miles, none of which is included in the area of Presidency Division.

Crops and Manufactures.—Rice is the staple crop, but considerable quantities of *wheat, jute, tobacco, indigo*, and *sugar cane* are also grown. Large quantities of *vegetables* and *condiments* are grown for the Calcutta market in the neighbouring districts. The *date* tree is extensively cultivated in Jessore, Khulna, and parts of Nadia, and the twenty-four Parganas for the manufacture of *date-sugar*.

The chief manufactures of the Division are *cotton-twist* and *yarn*, *gunny bags* and *cloth*, *paper*, *ice*, *shellac*, and *lac-dye*, *indigo*, *silk*, *sugar* and *molasses*. These manufactures, except the four last, are only carried on in the twenty-four Parganas District, in and near Calcutta, and generally close to the river. In 1894, fifty-eight mills, presses, and factories were at work. *Indigo* is manufactured in the Districts of Nadia, Jessore, and Murshidābād.

The manufacture of *silk* is a considerable industry in Murshidābād District, and that of *sugar* in every District but this. There are English refineries at Cossipore, a suburb of Calcutta, and in several other places in the Division.

There are no mines or quarries in any part of the Division. The ordinary building materials are mud and bricks. The latter are made in great quantities on the banks of the river below Calcutta.

Internal Communications.—The Division is well supplied with road, railway, and water communications. The Eastern Bengal Railway has its terminus at Siāldah, an eastern suburb of Calcutta, and runs along the east bank of the Hooghly for nearly forty miles, after which it strikes north-east across the Division. From Poradāha, 103 miles from Calcutta, a branch goes to the Ganges at Dāmukdia, which is connected by steam ferry with Sāra on the opposite bank, the terminus of the metre-gauge railway of North Bengal. Another branch runs from Poradāha along the south bank of the Ganges to Goalando, at the junction of the Ganges and Brahmaputra, whence the Assam mail steamers start. From Dum-Dum, four miles from Siāldah, a branch proceeds to Jessore and Khulna, and another line from Siāldah goes to Diamond Harbour on the Hooghly, thirty-eight miles below Calcutta, with one branch to the Hooghly at Budge Budge, and another to the Matla at Port Canning.

There are also regular boat and steamer routes across the Division. The steamer route in the dry season is down the Hooghly to Saugor Island, thence by the creeks and rivers of the Sundarbans to Barisāl, and up the Ariāl Khān to Goalando, or on to the Meghna. In the rains steamers, as well as country boats, go up the Hooghly and Jalangi to the Ganges. The boat route through the Sundarbans is higher up than the steamer route. From Calcutta they go by Tolly's Nullah, or the Bāliāghāta canal, in the Bidyādhari river and the Matla. Thence they go by channels connecting the Matla, Jamuna, Kobadak, and Bhāirāb, to Khulna and the Mādhumati, after which they either go up the Mādhumati to the Ganges, or by Barisāl to the Ariāl Khān or Meghna.

Climate.—The climate of the Division is inter-

Observing Stations in Presidency Division.	Average Maximum temperatures in		Average Minimum Temperatures in		Mean Annual Rainfall in inches.
	January.	May.	January.	May.	
Calcutta	76·9	93·5	55·4	76·9	63·44
Saugor Island ..	76·6	91·5	59·4	80·5	73·09
Jessore	78·0	94·2	53·2	76·4	65·70
Krishnagar ...	77·8	96·5	51·7	76·3	58·34
Berhampore ...	76·8	95·7	53·3	76·0	57·41

mediate between the drier and hotter climate of Western Bengal, and the damper, cooler and more equable climate of Eastern Bengal. The districts of Nadia and Jessore have of late years suffered greatly from fever, and it may be noted that these are the districts in which free natural drainage has been most interfered with by the silting up of deltaic distributaries.

CALCUTTA.

Though geographically within the 24-Parganas, Calcutta ranks as a separate District. The settlement was founded by Job Charnock in 1686, when, owing to a quarrel with the Nawāb of Bengal, he was obliged to fly from Hooghly. The modern city, with its suburbs, occupies twenty square miles, and had in 1891 a population of 681,560, of which 28,997 were Christians. The total number of Europeans was 11,914, of whom 5,323 were European-born. The number of Eurasians was 9,818. Calcutta stands on the east or left bank of the Hooghly, here about half a mile wide, and the level of the country declines from the river to the salt lakes, a few miles east of the city. It is eighty-six miles from the sea, and has a river frontage of between five and six miles. The ships lie at moorings along the bank of the river two and three, and, sometimes, four deep. They discharge and take in cargo by lighters and country boats. There is also a line of jetties chiefly used by the larger steamers. Docks have recently been constructed at Kidderpore, south of the city, but hitherto have been little used. Calcutta is the second port in India, Bombay being the first. As a town Calcutta takes the first place in the east as regards the provision made for the physical well-being of its population. It has an extensive and almost complete drainage system, which conducts both sewage and surface drainage away from the river to the salt-lakes, where also the solid refuse of the town is carried, or burnt. The water supply is excellent, being pumped from the river above Barrackpore, and,

HINDU TEMPLE.

after filtration, conducted to Calcutta in iron mains, and distributed over the town. The streets are lighted with gas, and, altogether, Calcutta enjoys most of the conveniences of civilization. The northern portion of the town, which is the native quarter, is marked by the over-crowding and the narrow winding streets usually found in Eastern cities, but of late years broad streets have, in places, been driven through this part, and great improvements effected. The centre of the town is the official and business quarter, which concentrates itself near the river, south of the floating bridge connecting Calcutta with Howrah. Most of the southern portion of the town is occupied by the Maidān, a grassy, park-like expanse about two miles long. On this, commanding the river, stands Fort William, and, at the northern end of it, Government House, the Town Hall, and the High Court. Bordering the Maidān on the land side runs the well-known Chowringhee road, which, with the rest of the southern part of the town, constitutes the European quarter.

Calcutta, besides being the capital of Bengal, and the seat of the Provincial Government, is the metropolis of India and the cold-weather seat of the Viceroy and the Supreme Government. It has a municipality for the management of civic affairs, its own police, and its own petty civil and criminal courts. The High Court is a Court of Appeal for the whole province, besides holding Criminal Sessions for the trial of prisoners charged with serious offences committed within the district of Calcutta.

24-PARGANAS DISTRICT.

Area, 2,108 square miles, a little less than the North Riding of Yorkshire. Population, 1,892,033. In 1757, Mīr Jafar, Nawāb Nāzim of Bengal, ceded to the East India Company twenty-four *parganas* or revenue divisions, situated near Calcutta, having an area of about 882 square miles. These are included in the modern district, and have given it its name. The administrative headquarters of the district are at *Alipore*, a south-west suburb of Calcutta, where Warren Hastings and Philip Francis once lived. Belvidere, the official residence of the Lieutenant-Governor of Bengal, is here.

Barrackpore.—Population 56,627, is on the Hooghly, fifteen miles by river, and fourteen by rail from Calcutta. Here the Viceroy has a country house, standing in a beautifully laid-out park. It is a military cantonment, and a favourite place of residence for many people employed in Calcutta. This was one of the first places where the mutiny of 1857 showed itself.

Port Canning, on the Matla, twenty-eight miles from Calcutta, is the remains of an attempt to found a port auxiliary to Calcutta. Jetties, mills, and a hotel were built, now all neglected and going to ruin.

Morelganj, on a tributary of the Baleswar river, about thirty-five miles from the sea, was founded in 1849 by Messrs. Morell and Lightfoot, who bought a tract of the Sundarbans from the Government, and reclaimed it. The port is convenient and safe, and exports large quantities of rice.

NADIA DISTRICT.

Area: 2,793 square miles. Population: 1,644,108.

Krishnagar, population 25,500, on the Jalangi, is the District headquarters. The town is celebrated for its manufacture of coloured clay figures. The population has decreased by nearly 2,000 since 1871 owing to the ravages of fever.

Nadia, population 13,334, on the west or right bank of the Bhāgirathi, was the ancient capital of the

District. It is celebrated for its pandits, who impart Sanskrit learning to students in their *tols* or colleges.

Sāntipur, population 30,437, on the Hooghly, is the largest town in the District. It was formerly the centre of the East India Company's cloth manufacture.

MURSHIDĀBĀD DISTRICT.

Area: 2,143 square miles; a little larger than Norfolk. Population: 1,250,946.

Berhampore, population 23,515, on the left bank of the Bhāgirathi, about one hundred and sixty miles from Calcutta, is the District headquarters. It was formerly a large military station, owing to its proximity to Murshidābād, the Muhammedan capital of Bengal, but no troops are now kept there. The first outbreak of the mutiny of 1857 took place here.

Murshidābād, population 35,576, is on the Bhāgirathi, five miles north of Berhampore. Clive described the city as being "as extensive, populous, and rich as the city of London," but since Plassey it has lost all importance. The Nawāb, who is the lineal descendant of Mīr Jaffar, has his palace here. Murshidābād is the centre of the silk manufacture of the Division, but the industry is a declining one. Between the city and Berhampore are the remains of Cossimbuzar.

Jiāganj, on the left bank of the Bhāgirathi about three miles above Murshidābād, is the chief seat of trade in the District. It is exactly opposite the railway station of Azimganj, the terminus of a short branch of the East Indian Railway.

JESSORE DISTRICT.

Area: 2,925 square miles. Population: 1,888,827.

Jessore, population 8,302, the headquarters of the

BURDWĀN DIVISION

Scale 1 Inch = 48 Miles.

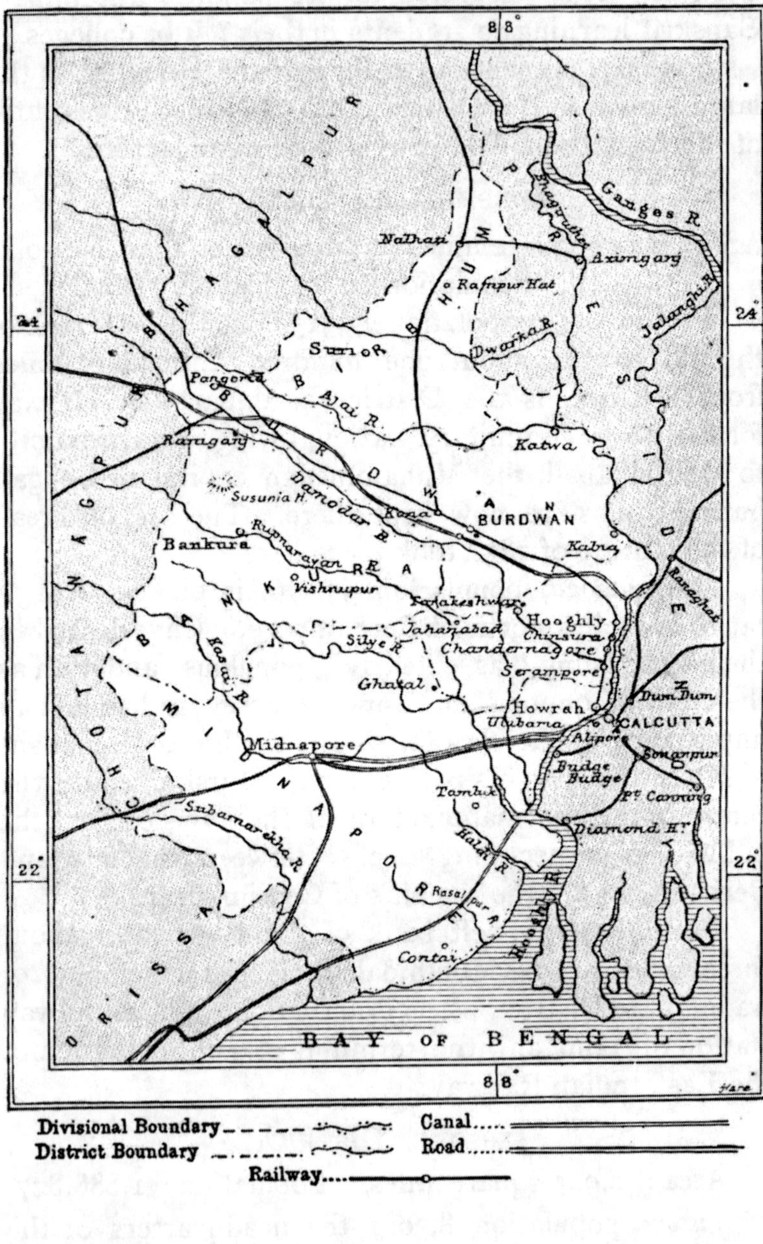

Divisional Boundary ....
District Boundary ....
Canal ....
Road ....
Railway ....

District, is directly connected by rail with Calcutta, distant seventy-five miles. The town is on the Bhāirāb, now an insignificant stream owing to the silting up of its head waters, but formerly the great central river of the District. A little below the town, where it comes under the influence of the tides, it is still a navigable river.

Kotchandpur, population 9,502, on the Kobadak, twenty-five miles north-west of Jessore, is the largest town of the District, and the chief seat of trade. It is a great date-sugar mart.

KHULNA DISTRICT.

Area: 2,077 square miles. Population: 1,177,652.

Khulna, population 8,667, situated on the Bhāirāb, where it meets the Sundarbans boat route, is the District headquarters. It is one hundred and ten miles by rail from Calcutta. It has been called the capital of the Sundarbans, and all the boat traffic from the east and north-east to Calcutta passes here. Steamers also ply, going north up the Chitra river past Narāil, and south-east through Bāgerhāt to Barisāl.

II. BURDWĀN DIVISION:

Area: 13,949 square miles. Population: 7,688,818.

Districts.	*Area.*	*Population.*
Burdwān	2,689 ...	1,391,880
Bīrbhum	1,752 ...	797,833
Bānkura	2,621 ...	1,069,668
Midnapore	5,186 ...	2,631,516
Hooghly	1,225 ...	1,076,710
Howrah	476 ...	721,211

Names, Boundaries, etc.—This Division takes its name from the town of Burdwān, which also gives its name to the District in which it is situated. In shape it is roughly quadrilateral, with a narrow strip in the north projecting between Bhāgalpur and Presidency Divisions. It is bounded on the north by the Districts of the Sonthāl Parganas and Murshidābād; on the east by the Districts of Nadia and the 24 Parganas, the boundary being the Bhāgirathi-Hooghly—except where, owing to a change in the course of the Bhāgirathi, Nadia town stands on a narrow strip on the Burdwān side of it; on the south by the Bay of Bengal and Balasore District; on the west by the Moharbhanj State, Mānbhum and Singbhum Districts. The Division is divided into six districts: Bīrbhum to the north; Burdwān south of this; further south Bānkura on the west, and Hooghly on the east; Howrah, south of Hooghly, and, south of all, Midnapore.

Size and Population.—The length of the Division is about 209 miles, and its breadth about 116 miles. Its area is 13,949 square miles, so that it is larger than Presidency Division by nearly 2,000 square miles. The population in 1891 was 7,688,818, less than that of Presidency Division by nearly a million, the number of persons to the square mile being 550. The District of Howrah is the smallest district of Bengal, and likewise the most densely populated, having 1,515 persons to the square mile. During the decade 1881-1891, the population of the Burdwān District has diminished by 2,343, owing to the ravages of the Burdwān fever, which has caused a material decrease of population since 1872. Bānkura and Bīrbhum are the most thinly populated districts. This is accounted for by the fact that the soil is only partially alluvial, and consequently less fertile. Of the total population of the Division over 80 per cent. are Hindus. About one million are Musalmāns, and nearly 300,000, chiefly found in the western parts of the Districts of Midnapore, Bānkura, and Bīrbhum, belong to aboriginal tribes.

3. *Physical Features.*—A glance at a map of fairly large scale shows a marked difference between Presidency Division and Burdwān Division: the latter has far fewer rivers and many more roads. The rivers are not the general highways of the country as they are in the delta. The eastern part of the Division is rich alluvial land. Where it borders upon the Hooghly it varies in elevation from 13 feet to 40 feet above sea-level, and has the character of deltaic country at a later period of its formation than the land east of the river. The *bīls* occupying the depressed tracts between the rivers have, in the majority of cases, silted up, and lost connection with them. The malarious nature of these parts is no doubt due to this stoppage of the natural drainage of the country, and, lately, attempts have been made to improve matters by re-opening connections with the rivers.

The south-eastern part of the Division, bordering upon the Hooghly and the sea, lies very low, and cultivation is only rendered possible by an extensive system of embankments to keep out river and sea. Proceeding west, the land rises, and the surface becomes undulating; only the hollows contain soil suitable for the cultivation of rice; while the higher ground is composed of beds of red laterite,* which

* Laterite is a porous clayey rock, largely impregnated with peroxide of iron irregularly distributed throughout the mass.

forms a highly infertile soil. In the west the country merges into the uplands of Moharbhanj and Chota Nāgpur, and, as we go north along the western border, there is a steady rise, until in the north of Bānkura we find jungle-clad hills upwards of 1,000 feet high. The best known of these hills is Susunia Hill, in the north-west of Bānkura District, which rises to 1,444 feet. Across the Dāmodar, in the coal country north-west of Burdwān District, the land is still fairly high, but the geological formation is different.

The hard beds of red laterite which occupy the western portion of this Division mark the limit of the great alluvial plain of Bengal. A line drawn in a northerly direction from the fringe of the laterite in Midnapore District passes over rich alluvial plain for upwards of 300 miles, only attaining an elevation of 300 feet near the base of the Himalaya.

The rivers of the Division are nearly all tributaries of the Hooghly having their origin in the highlands of Chota Nāgpur and the tributary states of Orissa. They have comparatively short courses, and are subject to rapid rises after rain in the hills. Of the more important of these the *Ajai* is the most northerly. It forms the boundary between Bīrbhum and Burdwān Districts, and flows into the Bhāgirathi at Katwa. The *Dāmodar* rises in Chota Nāgpur, and flows west, forming for some distance the boundary between Burdwān and Bānkura Districts. Past Burdwān town it turns sharply south, and joins the Hooghly opposite Falta about 30 miles below Calcutta. It is subject to sudden floods, from which the country is protected by an extensive system of Government embankments, and by the railway embankment which runs parallel to the course of the river through most of the district. South of the Dāmodar, through the middle of Bānkura District, flows the *Dakisor*, which, like the Dāmodar, takes a sharp turn to the south, and eventually joins the Hooghly as the *Rupnārāin* six miles below the Dāmodar. Between the mouths of the two rivers are formed the ill-famed "James and Mary" sands, so called from a ship which was swallowed by them at the end of the last century. The *Kasāi* flows through Midnapore District past the town of Midnapore, and after a tortuous course enters the estuary of the Hooghly as the *Haldi*.

Crops, Manufactures, Products.—Rice is the staple crop of the Division, the low-lying districts being remarkably fertile. The long stemmed variety is not grown. Other important crops are *potatoes*, which are largely grown in old river beds, *rape-seed, mustard, sugar-cane*, and *pāṇ* or betel leaf.

Silk is woven in most of the Districts, but it is a declining industry, and what is produced is a cheap material, chiefly sent up country. *Cotton-cloth* is also manufactured for local consumption, and the manufacture has of late received a stimulus, owing to the fall in the value of the rupee. *Gunny bags* and *cloth* are largely manufactured in the jute mills of Howrah and Serampore. *Brass* and *hardware* are extensively manufactured in Burdwān, Midnapore, and Hooghly. At Rāniganj are *paper* mills and *pottery* works, and at Howrah there are several *iron* works.

This Division possesses a great source of wealth in its coal-field at Rāniganj, which is about 30 miles long by 18 broad. There are also two collieries in Bānkura District. The total output in 1892-93 was over a million tons. The miners are drawn from the aboriginal races, chiefly Sonthāls and Bauris. *Lac* is found in the jungles of the western border, and there are lac factories in Bānkura and Bīrbhum Districts, where the dye is extracted from the natural product (called stick-lac), while *shellac* is prepared from the residue. Large quantities of *tussar-silk* cocoons are also collected in these jungles, and exported to Murshidābād for winding.

Internal Communications.—The main line of the East Indian Railway has its terminus at Howrah, opposite Calcutta, and runs along the right bank of the Hooghly through Serampore and Hooghly town. A little beyond Serampore a branch proceeds north-west across the Hooghly District to Tārākeswar, a celebrated place of pilgrimage. After passing Hooghly the line leaves the river, and crosses the Division in a north-west direction, through Burdwān town and Rāniganj. At Khāna, a few miles past Burdwān, a branch strikes off north, which goes through Bīrbhum towards the Ganges at Rājmahāl. At Assansol, a few miles beyond Rāniganj, the Bengal-Nāgpur Railway branches off.

The Division is well supplied with roads. The Grand Trunk Road to the North West Provinces traverses the Division, following much the same line of route as the railway, and it is joined near Rāniganj by a road from the south, which passes through Midnapore and Bānkura.

The principal water highway of the Division is the Hooghly, which, "like a busy street, carries the overflowings of the wealth and population of Calcutta to the places along its banks, and brings back in return the produce of the district." A high level canal, 53 miles in length, joins the Hooghly with Midnapore, starting from Ulubāria, 16 miles below Calcutta. It is navigable by small steamers, and is also used for purposes of irrigation. There is also a tidal canal connecting the Rupnārāin river, near its mouth, with Balasore. This is intended for navigation only. The chief rivers traversing the Division are navigable during the rains, and throughout the year within the limits of tidal influence. The Ajai is the only important river which is unaffected by the tides.

Climate.—The eastern part of the Division has much the same climate as Presidency Division, but in the western portion, where the laterite formation occurs, the climate is much drier, and the hot season hotter.

Names of Observing Stations in Burdwān Division.	Average Maximum Temperatures.		Average Minimum Temperatures.		Mean Annual Rainfall, in inches.
	January.	May.	January.	May.	
Burdwān	78·5	97·2	54·7	77·2	54·89
Rāniganj	78·1	100·6	54·2	77·5	53·25
Bānkura	78·6	100·1	54·9	77·8	56·59
Midnapore ...	81·0	99·8	55·3	77·7	56·03

There has been much discussion as to the cause of the "Burdwān" fever, which has ravaged the eastern parts of the Division for so many years. It has been ascribed to the interference with the free natural drainage of the country by the silting-up of old river channels, and this is certainly a predisposing influence. Most natives of Burdwān believe it to be due to the railway embankment, which was constructed shortly before the time the fever first made its appearance. The latter opinion is not supported by scientific evidence, but the question is still an open one.

BURDWĀN DISTRICT.

Area: 2,689 square miles. Population: 1,391,880.

Burdwān town, population 34,477, is the head-quarters of the District, and also of the Division. It is 67 miles from Calcutta by the East Indian Railway. The town stands a little north of the Dāmodar river. The Maharajah of Burdwān has a palace here. Knives and scissors of good quality are made at Kanchannagar, a suburb of the town.

Rāniganj, population 13,772, on the Dāmodar, 54 miles from Burdwān by railway, is the centre of the coal industry. Large quantities of coal are sent down the river to the Hooghly in barges during the rains.

Katwa, population 6,699, at the confluence of the Ajai and Bhāgirathi, an important trade centre.

Kalna, population 9,680, on the Bhāgirathi, connected by a good road with Burdwān, is the chief river mart and commercial centre of the District.

BĪRBHUM DISTRICT.

Area: 1,752 square miles. Population: 797,833.

Suri, population 7,481, is the District head quarters. It stands on laterite soil in the eastern portion of the District, about 11 miles from Sāinthia, a railway station on the East Indian Railway loop line. No navigable river flows through the District.

BĀNKURA DISTRICT.

Area: 2,621 square miles. Population: 1,069,668.

Bānkura, population 18,743, is the District head-quarters, situated on the north bank of the Dakisor river, here not navigable, about 30 miles from Rāniganj railway station, with which it is connected by an excellent laterite road.

Vishnupur, population 18,190, about 20 miles south-east of Bānkura, is the seat of a considerable silk-weaving industry. Here are the ruins of the ancient capital of the Rajas of Vishnupur—a very old family, now reduced to poverty. Some of the ancient temples are in fair preservation.

MIDNAPORE DISTRICT.

Area: 5,186 square miles. Population: 2,631,516.

Midnapore, population 32,264, is the District head-quarters, situated about the centre of the District, on the Kasāi, here an insignificant stream except during the rains. The soil is laterite and the climate dry. Brass and copper utensils are manufactured in the town, and there are several stone quarries in the neighbourhood. There is a steamer service by canal and river between Midnapore and Calcutta.

Tamluk, population 6,612, is on the banks of the Rupnārāin, in the south-eastern part of the District. The place is chiefly interesting on account of its great antiquity. In the early part of the fifth century it was the capital of a Buddhist Kingdom, and was a great port, situated on the sea, which is now 60 miles distant. It was several times visited by Chinese travellers. Only a few ruins remain to attest its former grandeur.

Hooghly District.

Area: 1,225 square miles. Population: 1,076,710.

Hooghly with Chinsura, population 33,060, is the District head quarters, situated on the Hooghly, 24 miles by rail from Howrah. Hooghly is said to have

The Hooghly, near Chinsura.

been founded by the Portuguese in 1537, on the decay of Sātgāon, the royal port of Bengal, through the silting-up of the Saraswati river, which was then a main branch of the Ganges. At the present time Sātgāon, once a great city, is a small village, and the Saraswati is a shallow creek which branches off from the Hooghly about eight miles above Hooghly town. Hooghly was the first settlement of the English in Lower Bengal, having been established by the East India Company in 1640. In 1686, owing to disputes with the Nawāb of Bengal, the English factors took refuge at Calcutta. The first printing press in Bengal was set up here.

Chinsura, now part of Hooghly, was established by the Dutch in the seventeenth century, and was ceded to the English in exchange for Java in 1825.

Serampore, population 35,952, is situated on the Hooghly opposite Barrackpore. Until 1845 it was a Danish settlement. A celebrated Baptist Mission was founded here by Carey in 1799, part of the site of which is now occupied by a jute mill.

Chandernagore, the only remaining portion of French territory in Bengal, is situated on the Hooghly, a little below Chinsura. It was founded in 1673, and rose to importance under Dupleix. It was bombarded and captured by Admiral Watson in 1757. It has now no commercial importance.

Howrah District.

Area: 476 square miles. Population: 721,211.

Howrah, population 116,606, the District head-quarters, is situated on the Hooghly opposite Calcutta, with which it is connected by a pontoon bridge. It is practically part of Calcutta. There are iron works, jute and cotton mills, on the banks of the river. At Sibpur, a suburb to the south, is a Government En-

RĀJSHĀHI DIVISION

Scale 1 Inch = 48 Miles.

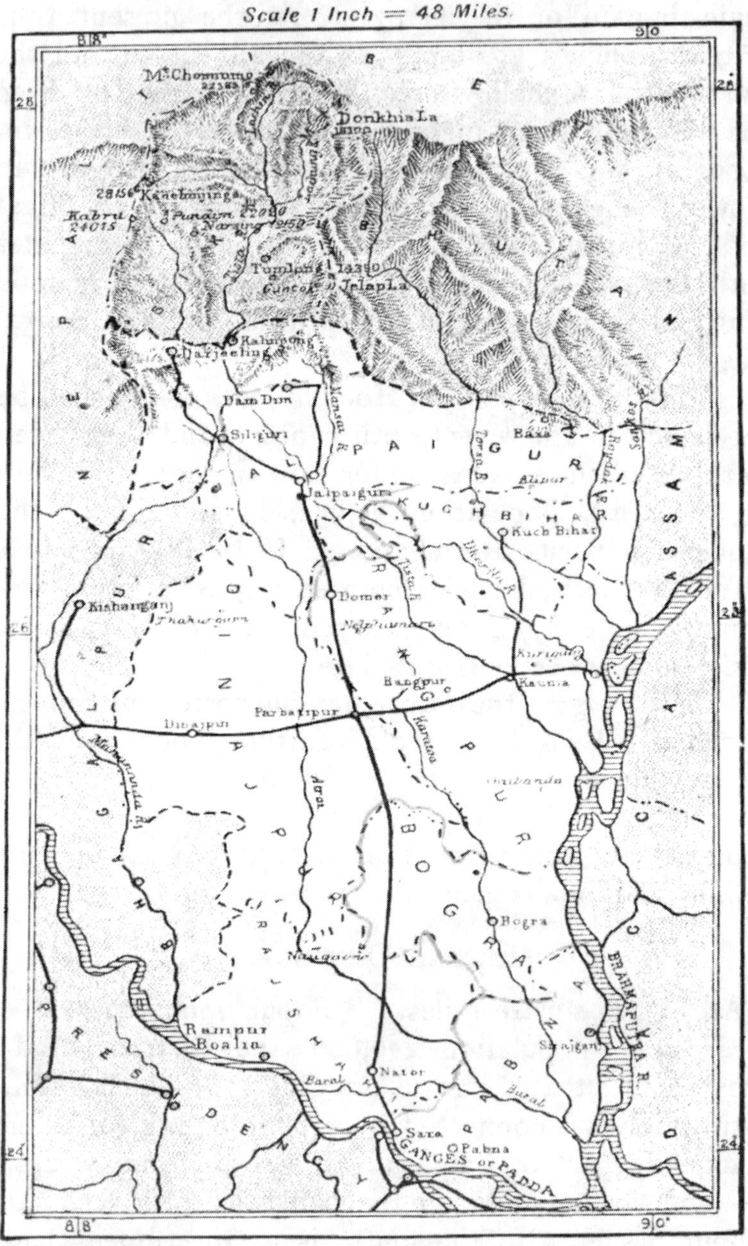

Divisional Boundary.......... — — —

District Boundary.......... — — - -

gineering College, and here also, on the banks of the river, are the Royal Botanic Gardens, which have a world-wide reputation. At Ulubāria, on the Hooghly, about 15 miles south of Howrah, the Midnapore canal leaves the river. A little above Ulubāria the Kāna Dāmodar joins the Hooghly. This small river represents the old channel of the Dāmodar, which changed its course about a century ago and now enters the Hooghly about 16 miles lower down.

III. Rājshāhi Division:

Area: 17,356 square miles. Population: 8,019,187.

Districts.	*Area.*	*Population.*
Rājshāhi	2,329 ...	1,313,336
Dinājpur	4,117 ...	1,555,835
Jalpāiguri	2,962 ...	681,352
Darjeeling	1,164 ...	223,314
Rangpur	3,493 ...	2,065,464
Bogra	1,452 ...	817,494
Pabna	1,839 ...	1,362,392
Native States.	*Area.*	*Population.*
Kuch-Bihār	1,307 ...	578,868
Sikkim	2,600 ...	30,458

Name, Boundaries, etc.—Until the Permanent Settlement in 1793, Rājshāhi was the most extensive *zamindāri** in Bengal, extending from Bhāgalpur in the west to Dācca in the east, and including considerable tracts now south of the Ganges.

* A zamindari is a tract of land over which the right to collect rents from the cultivators (rāiyats) has been granted by Government to an individual (the zamindar), in consideration of a fixed sum to be annually paid by him.

The dimensions of the ancient *zamindāri* indicate that at the time of its formation the Ganges still occupied what is now the channel of the Bhāgirathi, and had not broken away to the south-east, and cut the Rājshāhi *zamindāri* in two. This territory has undergone successive curtailments for convenience of administration, and the modern Division consists of the central and northern portions of the old Rājshāhi *zamindāri*, together with Dinājpur, Rangpur, and the more recently acquired Districts of Darjeeling and Jalpāiguri. The Native States of Kuch Bihār and Sikkim are included within its geographical limits. It is bounded on the north by Tibet and Bhutān; on the east by the Goalpāra District of Assam, Kuch Bihār State, the Gāro Hills District of Assam, Mymensingh and Dācca Districts, the Brahmaputra river separating the last three Districts and part of Goalpāra from the Division; on the south and south-west by the Ganges or Padda river, separating it from Faridpur, Nadia, and Murshidābād Districts; and on the west by Mālda and Purnea Districts and the independent Kingdom of Nepāl.

The Division is divided into seven Districts: Rājshāhi in the south-west, Dinājpur north of this, Jalpāiguri, and Darjeeling in the north, Rangpur south of Jalpāiguri, Bogra south of Rangpur, and Pabna in the south-east, bordering on the Ganges. The last three Districts have the Brahmaputra east of them.

Size and Population.—The greatest length of the Division from its south-eastern corner to the north of Sikkim is a little more than 300 miles; its greatest breadth is about 116 miles. The area of the Division is 17,356 square miles, or, including Sikkim and Kuch Bihār Native States, 21,263 square miles.

The population in 1891 was 8,019,187, or, if we include Sikkim and Kuch Bihār, 8,628,513. The most thickly populated districts are those bordering on the Ganges and Brahmaputra; Pabna, with 740 persons to the square mile, having the densest population. Darjeeling, with 191 persons to the square mile, is the most thinly populated District, as might be expected of a region largely composed of mountain and forest. Of the total population about 60 per cent. are Musalmāns. Nearly three millions are Hindus, and there are over seventy thousand Buddhists, belonging chiefly to the hill races of Darjeeling and Sikkim.

Physical Features.—Rājshāhi, from the Ganges to the foot of the Himalaya, is an immense alluvial plain, much intersected by rivers and streams, and having many swamps and marshes, some of great size. The country rises very gradually from the Ganges and the Brahmaputra to the foot of the hills. At the south-east corner of the Division, near the confluence of the Ganges and Brahmaputra, the elevation above mean sea level is 38 feet; at the south-west corner, on the Ganges, 128 feet. Proceeding north along the Brahmaputra the rise is more gradual than along the western border, so that the country has a slight tilt to the south, and a somewhat greater tilt to the east. Within 24 miles of the base of the hills, an elevation of about 300 feet is reached. The hills rise abruptly in steep, confused masses from the plains, into which densely wooded spurs project, and from Sukna, a station on the Darjeeling-Himalayan Railway, where the ascent into the hills really begins, the distance in a straight line to Senchal, a hill above Darjeeling 8,599 feet high, is only 15 miles, while Kanchinjinga, 28,150 feet high, the third highest known mountain in the world, is only 66 miles away.

The whole of Sikkim and Hill Darjeeling consists of steep mountains and deep valleys, forest clad up to 12,000 feet. The elevations increase towards the north, until all the peaks are well above the snow line. The country is shut in by the Cholā range on the east; on the west Kanchinjinga sends out a huge spur stretching 60 miles south to the plains; and peaks over 20,000 feet high continue the western boundary northwards. On the north Sikkim is walled in by mountain masses, which never fall below 15,000 feet. The lowest pass into Tibet in the north is 16,000 feet high, and the lowest pass through the eastern (the Cholā range) is over 14,000 feet. As seen from Darjeeling the snow mountains of northern Sikkim present the appearance of a continuous range dominated by Kanchinjinga; but this is a deception produced by distance. *Kanchinjinga*, 28,150 feet high, is on the Nepāl frontier, 46 miles away; *Kabru*, 24,015 feet, seen to the left of Kanchinjinga, is also on the Nepāl frontier, but six miles nearer; while *Jannu*, 25,300 feet, is actually in Nepāl. On the right of Kanchinjinga, *Pundim*, 22,020 feet, is 37 miles almost due north of Darjeeling; *Narsing*, 19,150 feet, the nearest snow mountain, is 33 miles away; while *Chomiumo*, 22,385 feet, *Kangchinjhau*, 22,720 feet, and *Donkhia*, 18,100 feet, are close to the northern frontier, more than 70 miles away.

The drainage from the glaciers and the lower slopes collects in the valleys to form streams whose waters eventually find their way into the *Tīsta*. This river is formed by the union of the *Lāchen* and *Lāchung* rivers, the former of which has its source in the Cholāmo lake in the extreme north of Sikkim. It receives the *Great Rangit* near Darjeeling, where it forms the boundary between Sikkim and Darjeeling District. It has a very rapid current, and bursts into the plains through a gorge in the hills about 18 miles south-east of Darjeeling. The Tīsta brings down the whole drainage of Sikkim, and being largely glacier-fed, its waters are singularly clear and cold. It is navigable almost immediately after leaving the hills, and it takes a course generally south-east to the Brahmaputra.

East of the Tīsta three other rivers, which drain the interior ranges, enter the Division from the hills, the *Torsa*, whose head waters are in the Chumbi valley in Tibet; the *Rāydak* and *Sankos*, which bring down the drainage of Bhutān. The two latter rivers flow direct to the Brahmaputra; the former used to join the Dharlla, but within the last few years it has changed its course and now flows into the Kāljāni, a tributary of the Rāydak.

The other rivers which enter the Division from the hills have their origin in the outer ranges, and receive no drainage from the interior. The chief of these are the *Jāldaka*, which after receiving various tributaries, becomes the *Mansāi*, afterwards the *Dharlla*, and flows into the Brahmaputra; and the *Kāljāni*. All these rivers are navigable up to the limits of cultivation below the hills. Higher up their courses are impeded by rocks and rapids. West of the Tīsta the *Mahānanda* rises in the hills south of Darjeeling, but leaves the Division after a short course in the plains.

Two rivers of importance have their origin below

the hills: the *Atrāi* and the *Karatoa*. The Atrāi flows south from Jalpāiguri District through Dinājpur, and, entering the Chalan Bīl in Rājshāhi District, discharges its waters from the southern end of the bīl into the *Baral*, an offshoot from the Ganges which flows to the Brahamputra. The Karatoa flows from Rangpur through Bogra and Pabna Districts to the Brahamputra. This river was formerly of great magnitude, but has been deteriorating for many years, owing to the diversion of its feeders in Rangpur District to the Tīsta and other streams.

The main streams of the Ganges and Brahmaputra border the Division on the south and south-east respectively, uniting at the south-east corner of Pabna District, which is here intersected by many cross streams between the two rivers, and has the character of a deltaic tract. At the junction of the two great rivers constant changes are being made in the configuration of the country, and the actual point of junction has moved several miles south during the last thirty years.

Owing to the friable nature of the soil, and the rapid current of the rivers which leave the hills, the rivers of this Division are very apt to change their courses, and the country is seamed with old river beds, often occupied by swamps or bīls. The Tīsta, which is specially remarkable for sudden and violent changes of course, up to the end of last century joined the Atrāi and flowed to the Ganges; but in the disastrous floods of 1787 it burst across country to the Brahmaputra, of which river it has since been a tributary.

The general aspect of the Division in the plains, is that of other parts of the plains of Bengal: "broad

Photograph by] ELEPHANTS CROSSING THE TORSA. [*Bourne & Shepherd, Calcutta.*

expanses of low-lying rice land, studded with villages and hamlets embedded in groves of trees." Parts of Rājshāhi, Dinājpur, and the north-west of Bogra, called the *Barind*, are exceptional, being composed of a stiff red clay with an undulating surface, covered for the most part with scrub jungle. This country resembles the Mādhupur jungle in Dācca Division; the courses of the rivers through these parts are well defined, and less liable to change.

The southern part of the Division, with the exception of the Barind, is remarkable for the number and size of the *bīls*, which are below the level of the river banks, and receive the drainage of the district. The largest of these is *Chalan Bīl*, in Rājshahi District, fed by the Atrai and other navigable rivers, which lose themselves in it. It discharges itself by the Baral, and other channels, into the Brahmaputra. It covers, in the rains, about 100 square miles, and is the home of immense numbers of wild duck and other game birds.

The strip of land fringing the base of the hills is called, in Darjeeling District, the *Tarāi* (damp), and in Jalpāiguri District the *Dwārs* (passes). It varies in width from ten to thirty miles. The soil is generally light, dry, and gravelly, and minor streams from the hills often disappear in it for some miles. This is the region of forest, principally *sāl*, the most valuable of Indian timber. Near the hills herds of wild elephants are still found, and the heavy grass and reed jungle is the home of the tiger and rhinoceros. Of late years many tracts under the hills have been cleared for tea gardens. The abundance of rain, together with a highly porous soil which carries off water rapidly, suits the plant well.

Crops, Manufactures, etc.—Besides rice and other

general crops, *jute, hemp, rape-seed,* and *mustard, sugar cane, tobacco,* and *potatoes* are staples. About 40 per cent. of the whole area under jute cultivation in Bengal is in this Division, and Sirājganj, in Pabna District, is one of the greatest jute marts. The whole of the hemp for the preparation of *ganja* is grown under Government supervision in a tract known as the "Ganja mahāl" (tract), which comprises parts of Rājshāhi, Bogra, and Dinājpur Districts. Tobacco is very largely grown, and has a great reputation for the excellence of its quality. A great deal is exported, especially to Burma.

The soil and climate of both the hill and *tarāi* parts of Darjeeling District and of the Dwārs, have proved most suitable for the tea plant, and the industry, though not of long standing, is firmly established. The number of gardens in 1893 was 367, and the outturn over 29 million pounds.

Cinchona is manufactured in large quantities at the Government cinchona plantation and factory at Rangbī, near Darjeeling. *Silk* and *indigo* are both still manufactured in Rājshāhi District, but the industries are declining. A large quantity of *sāl* and *sīsu* timber is cut and floated down from the forests in the Darjeeling and Jalpāiguri Districts, but much of the produce of the hill forests is not available except locally, owing to the absence of means of transport. *Copper* and *coal* are found in the hills, but are scarcely worked. The Government Kheddah department carries on its *elephant-catching* operations in the Dwār Forests, and during the last five years has captured 350 elephants. The average price fetched by a full-sized elephant was Rs. 863.

Internal Communications.—The rivers of this Division, though generally navigable, cannot be described as the highways of the country, as they are in some parts, except in Pabna District, which has all the characters of recent deltaic land. None of the rivers are subject to tidal influence. The Ganges and Brahmaputra are navigated by inland steamers. The roads, though numerous, are mostly unmetalled, and cannot compare with the admirable laterite roads of the Burdwān Division.

The Northern Bengal Railway, a metre-gauge line, starts from Sāra on the Ganges, and runs north through the middle of the Division to Siliguri, near the foot of the hills, a distance of 196 miles, whence a line of two-foot gauge, 51 miles long, climbs the hills to Darjeeling. At Pārbatipur, 111 miles from Sāra, a branch proceeds west through Dinājpur into Purnea District, with a terminus on the Ganges at Manihāri, and another branch proceeds east through Rangpur to Kāunia on the Tīsta. From the opposite bank of the Tīsta two lines of smaller gauge go to the banks of the Dharlla river, one north to Mogal Hāt, and onward from the opposite bank of the Dharlla to Kuch Bihār; the other east to the Dharlla, and on from the opposite bank to Jatrāpur, on the Brahmaputra, where the Assam steamers from Goalando pick up the mails. From the Tīsta, opposite Jalpāiguri, a line runs north through the tea gardens of the Dwārs to Dam-Dim under the hills.

The trade in the hill country of Darjeeling and Sikkim is mostly carried on by means of small pack ponies, which carry their burdens along mountain roads that often descend in Darjeeling and Lower Sikkim to below a thousand feet, and again rise to four and five.

thousand. Towards the frontier passes into Tibet the elevations gradually increase, and the Jelap Lā pass, which is most in use, is 14,396 feet high. *Gold*, *wool*, *yak-tails*, *musk* and *ponies* are the chief imports from Tibet; while, in return, *manufactured cotton* and *wool*, and *indigo* are chiefly taken.

Climate.—This Division has a higher rainfall and a cooler and damper climate than Presidency Division.

Observing Stations in Rājshāhi Division.	Average Maximum Temperatures		Average Minimum Temperatures.		Mean Annual Rainfall in inches.
	January.	May.	January.	May.	
Rāmpur Boalia ...	75·3	93·7	50·5	75·2	58·19
Bogra	75·7	92·2	51·6	74·2	68·00
Dinājpur	75·3	91·1	49·2	73·7	69·55
Rangpur	74·5	88·9	49·3	72·1	82·81
Sirājganj	75·8	90·4	51·0	73·9	61·16
Jalpāiguri	73·1	87·6	50·7	71·1	127·41
Dārjeeling	45·0	62·7	34·6	50·7	120·8

It appears from the table that, as regards "plains" stations, the temperature decreases as the rainfall increases. The differences of temperature between different stations are least during the rains. Jalpāiguri, Rangpur, and Rājshāhi Districts are feverish, while the Tarāi and Dwārs are notoriously unhealthy.

Districts and Chief Towns.—The Rājshāhi Division is not one of great towns. It has no town with a population of 25,000.

RĀJSHĀHI DISTRICT.

Area: 2,329 square miles. Population: 1,313,336.

The District head quarters is Rāmpur Boalia, population 21,407, situated on the north bank of the Ganges.

It is a town of comparatively recent origin, and an important but declining commercial centre. It is very liable to the encroachments of the river, which has on several occasions threatened its existence. There are large silk factories near the station.

Nator is the ancient capital of the District, and the seat of the Rajahs of that name. On account of the unhealthiness of the place, the District head quarters were, in 18[illegible]5, removed to Rāmpur Boalia.

DINĀJPUR DISTRICT.

Area: 4,117 square miles. Population: 1,555,835.

Dinājpur, population 12,204, the District head-quarters, is situated on the branch railway, 23 miles west from Pārbatipur, an important railway junction in the District.

JALPĀIGURI DISTRICT.

Area: 2,962 square miles. Population: 681,352.

Jalpāiguri, population 9,682, situated on the west bank of the Tīsta, is the head-quarters of the District, and also of the Division. It is a railway station, 23 miles from Siliguri and 173 from Sāra. It is the centre of the Dwārs tea industry, and the new railway to Dam-Dim from the opposite bank of the Tīsta was made in the interests of the tea planters.

Baxa is a military outpost, in the lower range of the Bhutān hills, about 32 miles north of Kuch Bihār. A wing of a native regiment is stationed here.

DARJEELING DISTRICT.

Area: 1,164 square miles. Population: 223,314.

Darjeeling, population 14,145, the head-quarters of

Photograph by] [*Johnston & Hoffman, Calcutta.*

SNOWY RANGE ABOVE DARJEELING, FROM THE RAILWAY AND CART ROAD.

the District, and the chief hill station of Bengal, occupies a narrow ridge which rises steeply from the bed of the Great Rangit River to the north of it. It varies in height from 6,500 to 7,500 feet, and commands a magnificent view of the snowy range. The station was established in 1840, and affords a cool and healthy retreat for Europeans from the heat of the plains. It is the hot weather seat of the Bengal Government. There are many tea gardens near the station, which is connected by a railway 51 miles in length with Siliguri at the foot of the hills, the terminus of the Northern Bengal Railway. Siliguri is the centre of the Tarāi tea industry.

RANGPUR DISTRICT.

Area: 3,493 square miles. Population: 2,065,464.

Rangpur, population 14,216, is the head-quarters town. It has a station on the eastern branch of the Northern Bengal Railway, of which the terminus is Kāunia, on the banks of the Tīsta, 33 miles from Pārbatipur.

BOGRA DISTRICT.

Area: 1,452 square miles. Population: 817,494.

Bogra, population 6,584, on the Karatoa river, is the head-quarters town, and possesses no other importance.

PABNA DISTRICT.

Area: 1,839 square miles. Population: 1,362,392.

Pabna, population 16,486, the District head-quarters, is on the Ichchamati, an offshoot of the Ganges, which flows to the Brahmaputra.

Sirājganj, population 23,267, on the Brahmaputra,

is perhaps the most frequented river mart in Bengal, both for steamers and native boats. There is an immense trade in jute.

Native States.

SIKKIM.

Area: 2,600 square miles. Population: 30,458.

Tumlong, about 64 miles from Darjeeling, by rough mountain roads, was the capital and the chief residence of the Maharajah. Since the interference of the Indian Government in Sikkim affairs, Gantok, a village about eight miles south-east of Tumlong, has been made the residence of a British Political Agent, and the station of a wing of a regiment, and is practically the capital.

Gnatong, near the Tibetan frontier, north-east of Darjeeling, commands the road to the Jelap Lā pass. Part of a British regiment is stationed here in a rude fort, at an elevation of over 12,000 feet.

KUCH BIHĀR.

Area: 1,307 square miles. Population: 578,868.

Kuch Bihār, population 11,491, on the Torsa, is the chief town, and the residence of the Maharajah. It is connected by a railway 24 miles long with Mogal Hāt, on the banks of the Dharlla river. The best tobacco in Bengal is grown in the State, and is largely exported. Much jute is also grown. In its physical features the State resembles Jalpāiguri District, by which it is almost entirely surrounded.

DĀCCA DIVISION

Scale 1 Inch = 48 Miles.

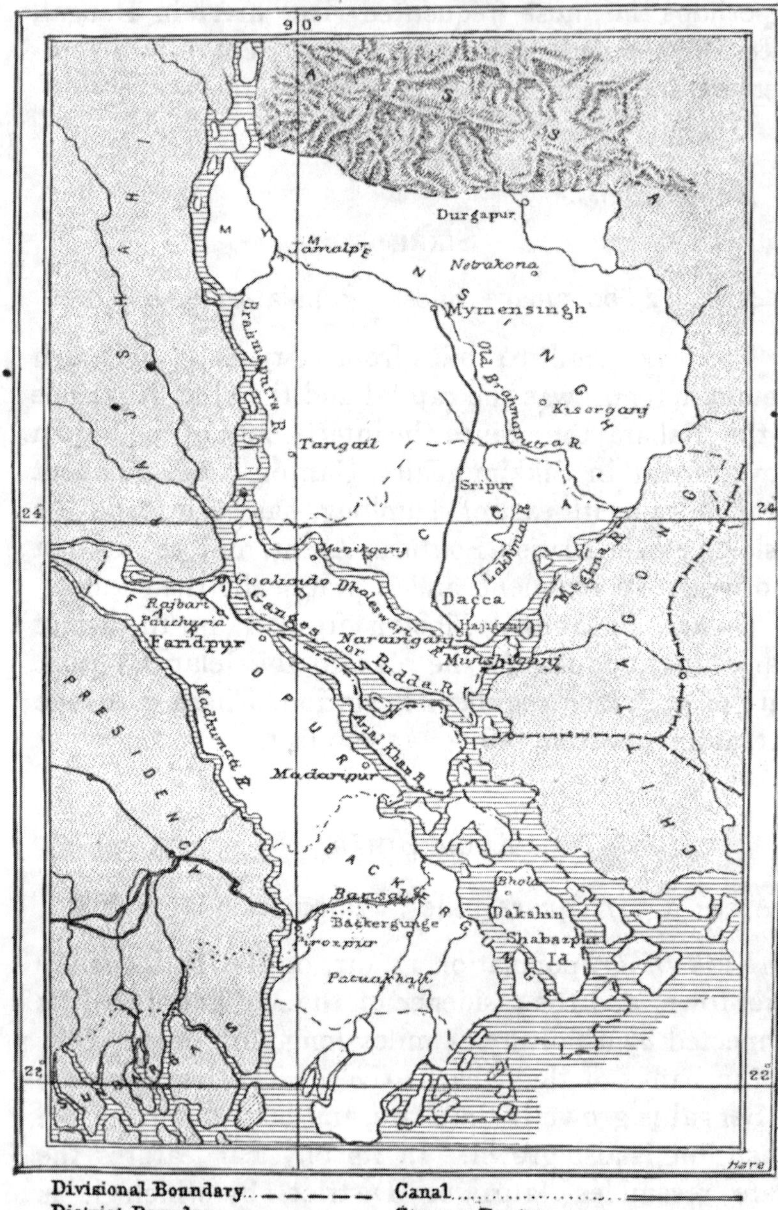

Divisional Boundary..........
District Boundary..........
Proposed Railway..........
Canal..........
Steamer Routes..........

IV. DĀCCA DIVISION:

Area: 15,040 square miles. Population: 9,844,127.

Districts.	*Area.*	*Population.*
Dācca	2,796	2,420,656
Mymensingh	6,332	3,472,186
Faridpur	2,267	1,797,320
Backergunge	3,645	2,153,9655

Boundaries, etc.—This Division is bounded on the north by the Gāro Hills in Assam; on the east by Sylhet District in Assam, and by Tippera and Noakhāli Districts; on the south by the Bay of Bengal; and on the west by Khulna, Jessore, Pabna, Bogra, and Rangpur Districts. The western boundary is, for the most part, the Brahmaputra, and, from a point south of its junction with the Ganges to the sea, the Mādhumati river; the Meghna constitutes the greater part of the eastern boundary. The Division is divided into four Districts in the following order from north to south: Mymensingh, Dācca, Faridpur, Bāckergunge. The last comprises the island of Dakhīn Shābāzpur, in the Meghna estuary, as well as numerous smaller islands or chars.

Size and Population.—The length is about 253 miles, and its greatest breadth about 110 miles. Its area is 15,040 square miles. The population in 1891 was 9,844,127, or 654 to the square mile, showing an increase of over a million since the previous census. Roughly, two-thirds of the population are Musalmāns, and one-third Hindus. The condition of the people is much more prosperous than in western Bengal and Bihār, and has improved of late years, owing to the jute industry.

The floating population is larger than in any other Division, numbering over 100,000.

Physical Features.—This Division is the meeting place of three great river systems, and in it we see, in highest activity, the work of rivers in making land and in changing its configuration. The main streams of the Ganges and Brahmaputra unite at Goalando in the north-east corner of Faridpur District; their combined waters receive the Meghna at the south-east corner of Dācca District, and the whole country is intersected by the subsidiary branches and tributaries of the great system thus formed. The Ganges divides the Division into two parts. In the northern part the surface of the country has a tilt to the east and south, the elevation falling along the course of the Brahmaputra from between 60 and 70 feet in the north-west corner to 21 feet in the south-west, the general line of drainage being towards the south-east. A curious exception to the general lie of the country is the Mādhupur jungle, an upland forest, practically uninhabited, averaging in height some 60 feet above the level of the plains. It runs north and south through Mymensingh and part of Dācca Districts for 45 miles, with a width varying from 6 to 16 miles. The soil of this tract is a red clay, largely impregnated with iron.

In the southern part of the Division the general surface level declines from an elevation of 27 feet near Goalando, to the Bāckergunge Sundarbans and the sea. This part of the Sundarbans is now practically all cleared, and is protected from the inundation of the sea by a line of sandhills which fringes the coast.

The whole Division, with the exception of most of the northern District of Mymensingh and the north-western part of Dācca District, is typical delta. Roads hardly exist, and all through the year boats form the vehicles of commerce and transit. The country is annually inundated by the overflow of the great rivers, and, at this time of year, boats ply over the country in every direction through the long-stemmed rice, which grows in water up to 20 feet in depth. The villages, surrounded by plantations of palms and bamboos, are built upon mounds of earth raised above flood-level, or occupy the banks of rivers, which are, as in all deltaic tracts, the highest part of the country. After the rainy season is over the land dries up, except the permanent swamps or *bīls*, which occupy the low land between the rivers and eventually drain into them.

The northern portion of the Division, though intersected by numerous rivers freely navigable at all periods of the year, is, except in the rainy season, practically a dry land, and is well supplied with roads.

The river system of the Division is so complex that it is impossible to do more than describe its general features. The Statistical Account of Bengal gives a list of no less than 61 separately-named rivers in the Bākergunge District alone, all navigable by craft of 50 tons burthen. All the rivers of the Division are of unstable character, and subject to continual change: some, like the Madhumati, increasing in size, others, especially in Mymensingh, silting up at their head waters and becoming what are known as "dead" rivers.

The Ganges borders Faridpur District as far as Goalando, where it receives the Brahmaputra, and enters the Division. It flows south-east from Goalando, separating Faridpur from Dācca District, and is joined by the Meghna opposite Chāndpur, in Tippera District.

These great rivers bring down enormous quantities of silt-laden water during the rainy season, and are constantly shifting their channels, making land at one place and destroying it at another. This action is especially violent at the confluence of the Ganges and the Brahmaputra, and the tongue of land on which Goalando and the terminus of the Eastern Bengal Railway are usually shown in the maps has long been transferred to the Pabna side of the river, and the present Goalando, instead of being nearly ten miles distant from the next station inland, is only about three miles from it. Similar changes in greater or less degree occur along the whole course of these rivers to the sea, and the islands of the Meghna estuary are particularly liable to sudden and violent changes of configuration, the general tendency being to destroy land at their northern extremities, and re-make it further south.

The following are the chief minor rivers: The old Brahmaputra flows in a south-easterly direction across the Mymensingh District to the Meghna. It takes off from the main Brahmaputra nearly opposite the mouth of the Tīsta. Less than a century ago this was the main Brahmaputra but within this period the big river has broken its way south by the channel of the Jamuna, formerly a minor river, and has left its old channel occupied by a dying river. The Lakmia river branches off from the old Brahmaputra at the northern boundary of Dācca District, and takes a southerly course to the Dhaleswari river, which it joins about four miles from its junction with the Meghna. The part of Dācca District west of the Lakmia differs considerably from the eastern and southern parts, lying comparatively high, and above flood-level. The soil is a red clay, and the channel of the river is well-defined and less shifting. Its banks are high and well-wooded. . The Dhaleswari river intersects Dācca District, brahching off from the Brahmaputra about 15 miles above its junction with the Ganges. It has a south-easterly course, and joins the Meghna at Munshiganj, about eight miles above its junction with the combined Ganges and Brahmaputra. The District south of this river is annually flooded.

In the part of the Division south of the Ganges the principal river is the Mādhumati, which is, except for a few miles in the north, the boundary between this and Presidency Division, under which it has been described. The Ariāl Khān leaves the Ganges a little below Faridpur town, and takes a course generally south-east to the Meghna estuary. It is a big river, which receives a number of tributaries, and sends off several offshoots during its course. It forms part of the Sundarbans steamer route from Calcutta to Goalando. All these rivers, especially those with comparatively open connection with the Meghna, are affected by the tide to a distance of about 100 miles from the sea, though, during the rains, when the rivers are in flood, the effect is not very marked. The tide does not reach as far as Goalando; at Dācca, on the Buriganga, an offshoot from the Dhaleswari, there is a rise and fall of about two feet during the dry season, while, in the island of Dakhīn Shābāzpur, creeks that are almost dry at low water have 18 or 19 feet of water at flood tide.

Crops, Manufactures, Products.—Besides rice, of which the long-stemmed variety is largely grown, the chief crop is *jute*, which is 37 per cent. of the total crop of the Province, and, owing to its cultivation, the great and increasing prosperity of the Division is largely due. *Chillies* and *betel-nuts* are also largely grown, and cocoanut plantations are very numerous, generally about the villages. There are no large manufactures. *Jute pressing* is carried on at Nārāyanganj ; *date-sugar* and *molasses* are manufactured in Faridpur District; and *boats* are built all over the Division. There are several *flour* and *oil* mills. Considerable quantities of *country cloth* are made, but the famous Dācca *muslins* are a thing of the past. There are no mines or quarries in the Division.

Internal Communications.—The rivers are the ordinary highways over the greater part of the Division. Every cultivator has his boat, which is his cart, and south of the Dhaleswari river, during the rainy season, the country can be crossed in almost every direction, the boats being poled along through the rice by long bamboos. North of the Dhaleswari the land is higher, and there are several main roads traversing the country. Inland steamers ply on the larger rivers. The Sundarbans steamer route from Calcutta passes Barisāl, and continues up the Ariāl Khān and the Ganges to Goalando, the terminus of the Eastern Bengal Railway, whence the mail steamers proceed up the Brahmaputra to Assam. Other steamers connect Goalando with Nārāyanganj on the Lakmia river, and proceed up the Meghna to the tea districts of Sylhet and Cachār. Another service of steamers plies between Khulna, Barisāl, Bhola, in the island of Dakhīn Shābāzpur, and Noākhāli. A railway connects Nārāyanganj, Dācca, and Mymensingh, which brings down enormous quantities of jute for shipment from Nārāyanganj.

Climate.—The climate of the Division is damp and equable. It is comparatively free from the malarial fever which has of late years devastated so many districts of Bengal, owing, no doubt, to the thorough flushing which the country gets every rainy season. Nearly all the rivers flow throughout the year, and afford an ample and pure water supply. The Division is, however, subject to outbreaks of cholera.

Names of Observing Stations in Dācca Division.	Average Maximum Temperatures in		Average Minimum Temperatures in		Mean Annual Rainfall in inches.
	January.	May.	January.	May.	
Dācca	78·2	90·8	55	75·5	71·83
Mymensingh ...	74·5	88·3	52·4	73·5	86·12
Faridpur	74·1	90·9	53	74·9	69·11
Barisāl	76·5	91·1	55	76·6	78·63

DĀCCA DISTRICT.

Area: 2,796 square miles, a little greater than the West Riding of Yorkshire. Population: 2,420,656, also almost the same as that of the West Riding, which is 2,439,895.

Dācca, population 82,321, is the headquarters of the District of that name, and of the Division. It is situated on the Buriganga, a loop of the Dhaleswari, and extends along the bank of the river for about 4 miles. It is the fourth largest city in Bengal. During the 17th century it was the Muhammedan capital of the Province, but it preserves few traces of its former importance. It ceased to be the capital in 1704, on the removal of the Nawāb of Bengal to Murshidābād. Dācca is favourably situated to command the three river systems of the Division.

THE BURIGANGA AT DĀCCA (SHOWING THE NAWAB'S PALACE).

Nārāyanganj, population 17,715, the port of Dācca, is situated on the Lakmia river, a little above its junction with the Dhaleswāri. It is the river terminus of the Dācca-Mymensingh railway, by which it is 10 miles from Dācca. It is a great jute emporium, and has steamer services with Calcutta direct, with the railway station at Goalando, with the Assam valley, and with the tea districts of Sylhet and Cachār. There is also a considerable trade by means of country boats with Chittagong, which is the natural seaport of the Division.

MYMENSINGH DISTRICT.

Area: 6,332 square miles. Population: 3,472,186.

Nasirabād or Mymensingh, population 11,555, is the District headquarters. It is situated on the west bank of the old Brahmaputra, 76 miles by railway north of Dācca. The place is of no great commercial importance, as the river is here only navigable by large boats during the rains. Three other towns of the District have a greater population, and are more important trade centres: Tangail 17,973, Jamālpur 13,388, and Kisorganj 13,988. Tangail appears to have rapidly grown to importance. It was not even classed as a town before 1881, and is not mentioned in the Statistical Account of Bengal. Several of the minor towns have enormously increased in population within the last ten years, owing to the development of the jute industry.

FARIDPUR DISTRICT.

Area: 2,267 square miles. Population: 1,797,320.

Faridpur, population 10,774, the District headquarters, is situated on the south bank of the Ganges.

CHITTAGONG DIVISION

Scale 1 Inch = 48 Miles.

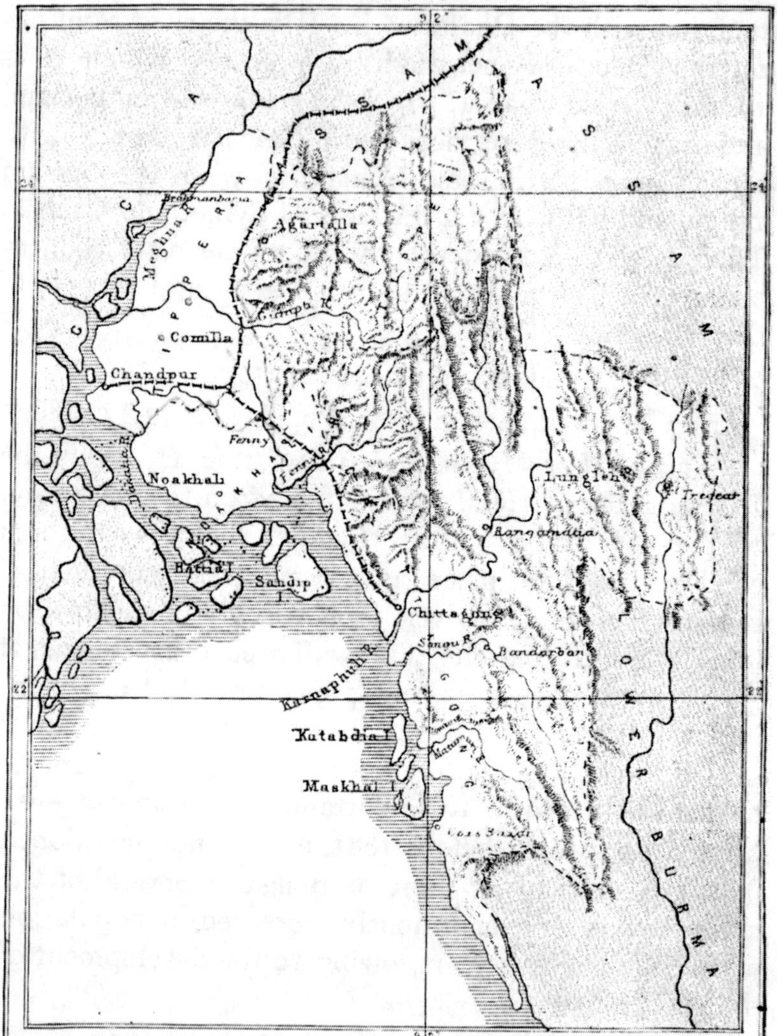

Divisional Boundary .... — — — — — —　　Railway under construction .... ┼┼┼┼┼┼

District Boundary .... —·—·—·—

It is connected by road with the Rājbāri station of the Eastern Bengal Railway. A deep fresh-water lake lies south of the town. In the rains most of the country is under water.

Madāripur, population 13,772, on the Ariāl Khān river in the south of the District, largely exports jute and sugar. It is proposed to cut a canal connecting this river with the Mādhumati at Gopālganj, west of Mādāripur. This would materially shorten the route to Khulna.

BĀCKERGUNGE DISTRICT.

Area : 3,645 square miles. Population : 2,153,965.

Barisāl, population 15,482, on the banks of the Barisāl river, an off-shoot of the Ariāl Khān, is the District headquarters. It is situated on the Sundarbans steamer route, and exports *rice, jute, betel-nuts, cocoa-nuts*, and *wood* from the Sundarbans forests.

Pīrojpur, population 12,248, on the Mādhumati, has grown to be the second town of the District since 1871.

V. CHITTAGONG DIVISION :

Area : 12,121 square miles. Population : 4,190,081.

Districts.	*Area.*		*Population.*
Tippera	2,491	...	1,782,935
Noākhāli	1,644	...	1,009,693
Chittagong (including the Hill Tracts)	7,986	...	1,397,453
South Lushāi Hills ...	2,400	...	10,000
Native States.	*Area.*		*Population.*
Hill Tippera	4,086	...	137,442

Name, Boundaries, Districts.—The town and district of Chittagong was ceded to the English in 1760, by Mīr Kāsim, the Nawāb of Bengal, together with Burdwān and Midnapore. It was long the head-quarters of Magh and half-caste Portuguese pirates, who used to ravage far up the rivers of Eastern Bengal, and carry into slavery the inhabitants of the river-side villages. The Division now comprised under the name consists of the mainland and islands at the head of the Bay of Bengal, east of the Meghna, and as far south as the Nāf river. It is bounded on the north by parts of Mymensingh and Sylhet, and by the native State of Hill Tippera; on the east by North Lushāi and Upper and Lower Burma; on the south by the Akyab District of Burma; on the west by the Bay of Bengal and the Meghna estuary and river. The independent native State of Hill Tippera, wedged in between Tippera and Chittagong Districts, with Sylhet and North Lushāi to the north and east, belongs geographically to this Division.

The Division is divided into four Districts: Tippera in the north-west; Noākhāli south of Tippera; Chittagong in the south; and the South Lushāi Hills District east of Chittagong. Hill Tippera lies east of Tippera and Noākhāli Districts.

Size and Population.—The greatest length of the Division from the north of Tippera to the south of Chittagong is about 266 miles, and its greatest breadth from west of Tippera to the east of South Lushāi about 175 miles. Its area, as given in the Census Report, is 12,121 square miles, which does not include the area of the South Lushāi District, about 2,400 square miles, hitherto unsurveyed, or that of Hill Tippera, 4,086 square miles. The population in 1891 was 4,190,181, or 345 to the square mile, showing an increase of over half a million since the census of 1881. It comprises nearly three millions of Musalmāns, about a million Hindus, and 137,269 Buddhists, out of 189,122 in the whole of Bengal.

The material condition of the population is good, except in the Hill Tracts. As a rule the people are better clad and more prosperous than in other parts of Bengal. Many of the Chittagongese are sailors, and form a large proportion of the lascars employed in the steamers trading in the east.

The great majority of the population of the Hill Tracts are Buddhists, consisting of two tribes, the Chakmas, and the Maghs, the latter being chiefly the descendants of immigrants from Burma in the first Burmese War. They practise in the hills the *jūm* method of cultivation, which consists in clearing a portion of jungle by fire, and planting a mixture of the seeds of cotton, rice, melons, pumpkins, yams, and a little Indian corn. This last ripens first; next melons and other vegetables, then, in September, the rice, and, last of all, in October, the cotton, which ends the harvest. A *jūm* is only cultivated one year; next year another *jūm* is made, and treated in the same way.

Physical Features.—Tippera, Noākhāli, and the strip of Chittagong about fifteen miles wide along the coast, have the general character of the rest of the Bengal delta. The country is rich alluvial plain, intersected by rivers and creeks, all more or less affected by the tide. The Division comprises a number of islands and *chars* in the Meghna estuary, of which the largest are Sandip and Hattia. Noākhāli and the islands of the Meghna have been formed by the silt brought down by the river, and every year changes take place, land being added at one place and washed away at another. The mainland of Noākhāli has been extending seawards for many years. Sometime in the last century the Meghna reached up to Noākhāli town, which is now eight miles distant from the river. The whole coast and islands of the Meghna are little above high-water mark, and are liable to be swept by storm waves. The worst in recent times was that which accompanied the cyclone of 1876, when the loss of life by drowning was very great, and the mortality from the cholera which followed equally excessive.

There are several islands off the coast of Chittagong, of which the largest are Kutabdia and Māskhāl. The latter is a pretty wooded island rising into low hills on the east side. The Chittagong coast is somewhat higher than that of Noākhāli, and rises as we proceed south.

In the eastern part of Tippera District a ridge averaging forty feet above the plains, and thickly wooded, runs north and south for about ten miles. The flat coast-strip of Chittagong is backed by low ranges of hills, which run mostly parallel with each other and the coast. The Sitākund range, containing the sacred peak of Sitākund, 1,155 feet in height, is the outermost range in the northern part of Chittagong District. It terminates near the town of Chittagong, north of the river Karnaphuli. The valley of the river Halda, a tributary of the Karnaphuli, separates this range from the next range to the east. South of the Karnaphuli the ranges nearest the coast are lower, the highest point, 880 feet, being reached in the tongue of land west of the Nāf river.

The inland part of the District, commonly known as the Chittagong Hill Tracts, is divided into four valleys, formed by its four principal rivers: the Fenny and the Karnaphuli, which flow transversely across the main line of the hills, and the Sangu and Mātāmuri, which run parallel to the ranges until they enter the plains, when they flow to the sea almost at right angles to their former courses. The Hill Tracts have been described as most difficult to pass through: a tangled mass of hill, ravine and cliff, covered with dense tree, bush, and creeper jungle. From the summits of the main ranges there is a magnificent view of apparently boundless forest. The highest point in these hills is 2,789 feet. The scenery up some of the rivers is very picturesque.

The physical features of Hill Tippera and the South Lushāi Hills District are very similar to those of the Chittagong Hill Tracts. The ranges, and also the valleys between them, increase in height as they approach the east; and the whole tract is a mass of hills, the ranges running north and south, covered with dense evergreen trees and bamboos, with open forests of pine and oak on the eastern side. Some of the peaks in South Lushāi rise to 8,000 feet.

The principal rivers which traverse the Division are the *Gumti* and *Dākātia*, which rise in Hill Tippera and Tippera respectively, and flow through Tippera district to the Meghna; the *Fenny*, which rises on the borders of Hill Tippera, and flows south, dividing that state from the Chittagong Hill Tracts, and then south-west to the Sandip channel of the Meghna, dividing

Noākhāli from Chittagong District; the *Karnaphuli*. the most important river of Chittagong, which rises in the South Lushāi Hills, and after a circuitous course southwards and westwards, falls into the Bay of Bengal twelve miles below the town of Chittagong, which is situated on its north bank; the *Sangu*, which rises in the Chittagong Hill Tracts, and takes a circuitous but generally northerly course for about 125 miles, after which it takes a tortuous westerly course through the plains, and falls into the Bay of Bengal, about ten miles south of the Kārnaphuli; the *Mātāmuri* which rises near the Sangu and flows parallel to it on the other side of a range of hills to the south for about 67 miles, after which it turns west through the plains, and enters the Bay of Bengal by several channels opposite the islands of Kutabdia and Māskhāl. All these rivers become rapid and deep during the rains.

The *Meghna,* which borders Tippera and Noākhāli, is joined, opposite Chāndpur, by the united streams of the Ganges and Brahmaputra. Its course is south, nowhere contained within clearly-defined banks, and it enters the sea by four principal mouths, of which the northern or Sandip channel is between Sandip Island and the mainland of Chittagong, and the one next south, the Hattia river, is between Sandip and Hattia islands. The Meghna is navigable by native boats of the largest burden, and also by river steamers, all the year through, but the navigation is difficult, and sometimes dangerous. Its sandbanks are constantly shifting, and the effect of the tides is very great. The regular rise of the tide is from ten to eighteen feet, and, at every new and full moon, a bore occurs, which is much dreaded by boatmen. At the equinoxes the navigation is sometimes impeded for days together, at which periods, particularly with a south wind, the bore comes up with a noise like thunder: a wall of water advancing with a velocity of 15 miles an hour, and a height of nearly 20 feet.

Crops, Manufactures, Products.—Besides rice, which is grown both in the plains and in the hill districts, the chief crops are *cotton*, *tobacco*, and, in Tippera, *jute*. The cultivation of cotton and tobacco is increasing, and considerable quantities are exported. *Timber* is a valuable product of the hill forests. It is floated down in logs, or brought down in boats during the rains, when the hill streams are full. *Tea* is a flourishing industry. There were 26 tea gardens in Chittagong in 1893. *Boat* and *ship building* are important industries. *Coal* is found in the hill country, but the quality is inferior.

Internal Communications.—The water highways are the chief means of communication in the Division. Nearly every village possesses water communication, and the majority of the inhabitants live more or less by river traffic. Some of the numerous creeks of the Chittagong coast have been artificially connected, and the line of communication thus formed is one of the chief highways of the District. The larger rivers are navigable throughout the year as far as the hills; within the hills the violence of the current during the rains makes them impracticable for large boats. The Karnaphuli is navigable by large sea-going ships and steamers as far as Chittagong, and great quantities of produce, especially jute, are brought down the Meghna for shipment from that port. Communication between Chittagong and the other Districts of the Division is maintained by steamers or sailing vessels. The roads of the Division are all unmetalled. The most important is the Dācca Trunk road, which runs from Chittagong to Comilla, and thence to the Meghna. A railway is under construction which will connect Chittagong with Comilla and Assam, with a branch to Chāndpur in Tippera District, at the junction of the Ganges and Meghna rivers.

Climate.—The climate is moist and equable. The annual rainfall of both Chittagong and Noākhāli Districts is over a hundred inches, and of Tippera somewhat less. Chittagong District is very unhealthy, malarious fever being common, aud cholera hardly ever absent. Noākhāli is also a feverish district, while Tippera is comparatively healthy.

Observing Stations in Chittagong Division.	Average Maximum Temperatures in		Average Minimum Temperatures in		Mean Annual Rainfall in inches.
	January.	May.	January.	May.	
Chittagong ...	77·8	88·0	55·4	75·1	104·94
Noakhali	77·3	88·5	52·7	75·7	121·57
Comilla	78·2	90·0	53·0	74·8	91·63

TIPPERA DISTRICT.

Area: 2,491 square miles, the size of co. Galway.
Population: 1,782,935.

Comilla, population 14,680, is the District head-quarters. The town is situated on the south bank of the Gumti, which, as the name implies, is very winding. In the rains the river often rises several feet above the level of the town, which is protected by embankments from inundation. Owing to the gradual rise of the bed of the river it was thought necessary to check it by opening

SCENE IN HILL TIPPERA.

Photograph by H.H. the Bara Thakur, of Hill Tippera.

the embankment at a point below the town. This was done a few years ago with good result. The town has always been very healthy, although from its situation the soil must be perfectly water-logged in the rainy season.

Chāndpur, on the Meghna, is the western terminus of the new railway, and a steamer station.

NOĀKHĀLI DISTRICT.

Area: 1,644 square miles, the size of Somerset.
Population: 1,009,693.

Noākhāli, population 5,479, is the District headquarters, situated near a creek communicating with the Meghna, which is about ten miles distant. The bore rushes up the creek and past the town during the rains.

CHITTAGONG DISTRICT.

Area (excluding the Hill Tracts): 2,567 square miles.
Population: 1,290,167.

Chittagong Hill Tracts. Area: 5,419 square miles. Population: 107,286.

Chittagong, population 24,069, situated on the right bank of the Karnaphuli, about twelve miles from its mouth, is an important and rising port. The river is convenient, and vessels can get up to the wharves in one tide. When the Assam-Chittagong railway is completed, it is anticipated that most of the produce of Eastern Bengal and Assam, of which Chittagong is the natural port, will be brought here for shipment. There is a weekly steamer service with Calcutta, 376 miles distant, and a considerable coasting trade by sailing vessels. The houses of the European residents of Chittagong are situated on a number of small, very steep little hills, each house on a separate hill. The town is now notorously unhealthy, and yet a century ago it was regarded as a sanatorium for Europeans. Sir William Jones had a house here, to which he used to retire occasionally from Calcutta. Its present unhealthiness is ascribed to the number of stagnant pools in the neighbourhood, and to the recently-formed mud banks in the river, which are to windward of the town, and exposed at low water.

Cox's Bazar, population 4,347, situated on the coast about 64 miles south of Chittagong, was originally a Magh settlement, and three-fourths of the population still are Buddists. The town and its inhabitants are quite unlike Bengal. The houses are built of timber, raised on piles, after the Burmese fashion. A beautiful beach of firm sand extends for miles, and the sea supplies a great variety of excellent fish, including oysters and soles.

Rangāmati, population 2,336, the headquarters of the Chittagong Hill Tracts, is pleasantly situated on the Karnaphuli, about 60 miles above Chittagong. Though within the hills its elevation is only 142 feet, as it stands on the river.

Bandārban is the largest place in the Hill Tracts, situated on the Sangu river, near where it leaves the hills.

SOUTH LUSHĀI HILLS DISTRICT.

Area: About 2,400 square miles. Population: About 10,000.

This tract was added to Bengal in 1891, after the military operations undertaken to put an end to the raids of the Lushāis. Another expedition was made through the country in 1892-1893, which met with no resistance, and the country seems to be settling down.

The headquarters of the District are at Lungleh, 3,500 feet above sea level, while Fort Tregear, the principal outpost, is situated at an elevation of nearly 4,800 feet. The District will probably be transferred to Assam.

Hill Tippera Tributary State.

Area: 4,086 square miles, the size of Inverness. Population: 137,442, being 47,321 in excess of that of the Scotch county. More than 100 square miles in the interior are believed to be uninhabited. The principal trade is in cotton and timber.

Agartala, 38 miles north of Comilla, is the capital, and residence of the Raja.

BIHĀR.

Area: 44,197 square miles. Population. 24,393,504.

I. Patna Division:

Area: 23,686 square miles. Population: 15,811,014.

Districts.	*Area.*	*Population.*
Patna	2,075	1,769,004
Gāya	4,712	2,138,331
Shāhābād	4,373	2,063,337
Darbhanga	3,335	2,801,955
Muzaffarpur	3,004	2,711,445
Sāran	2,656	2,467,477
Champāran	3,531	1,859,465

This, the north-western Division of the Province, is bounded on the north by Nepāl; on the east by Bhāgalpur and Monghyr; on the south by Hazāribāgh and Palāmau Districts in Chota Nāgpur; and on the west by the Districts of Mirzapur, Benāres, Ghāzipur, Ballia, and Gorakhpur, in the North-West Provinces. The Karamnāsa, the cursed stream of Hindu mythology, the Ganges, and the Gogra form parts of the western boundary. The Division comprises seven Districts: Darbhanga, Muzaffarpur, Sāran, and Champāran, north of the Ganges; and Patna, Gāya, and Shāhābād, south of the Ganges.

Size and Population.—Patna is the largest Division of the Bengal Presidency, having an area of 23,686 square miles, more than twice that of Belgium. Its

PATNA DIVISION

Scale 1 Inch = 48 Miles.

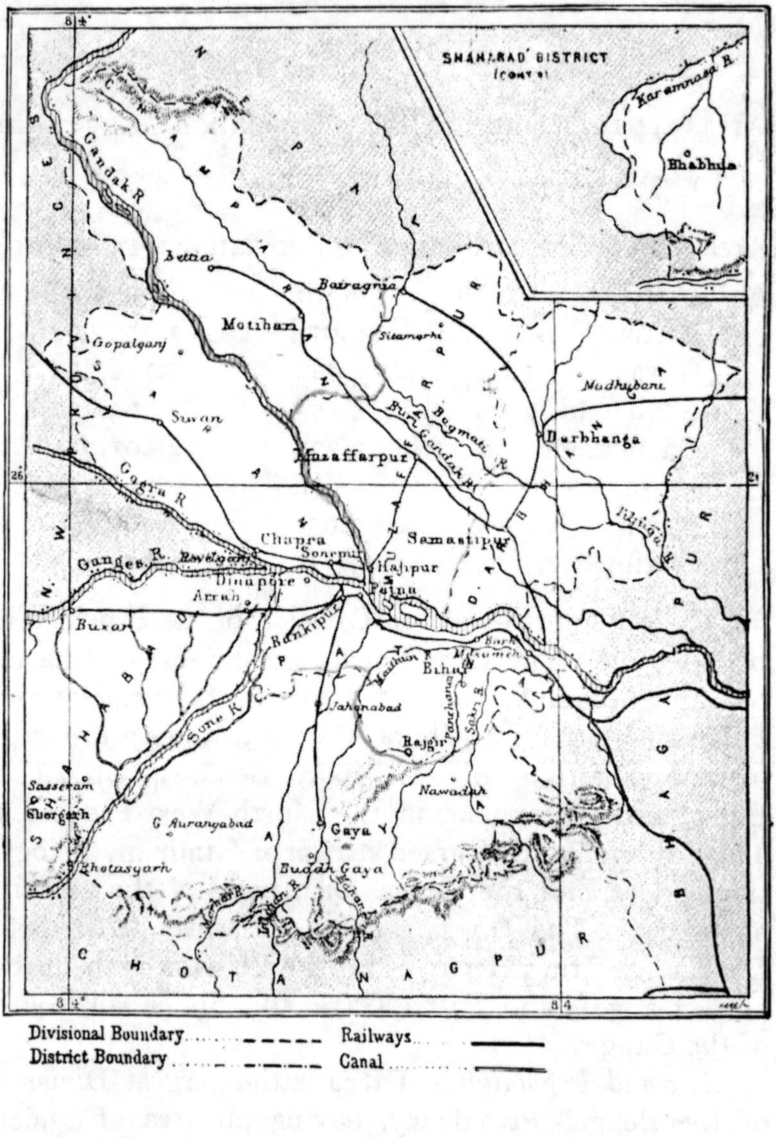

Divisional Boundary

District Boundary

Railways

Canal

greatest length from north to south is about 227 miles, and its greatest breadth from east to west about 178 miles, but the shape of the Division is extremely irregular. The population in 1891 was 15,811,014 (nearly equal to that of the whole Bombay Presidency), or 667 to the square mile; the adjoining Districts of Sāran and Muzaffarpur being the most densely populated, with 930 and 902 persons to the square mile respectively. The great majority of the population are Hindus, less than two millions being Musalmāns. Compared with eastern Bengal the mass of the people of this Division, especially in the southern Districts, are badly off, living more or less from hand to mouth, and being commonly in debt to usurers.

Physical Features.—The greater part of the Division is highly-cultivated alluvial plain, rising into wooded hills in the south, and also in the north-west, and divided by the Ganges into two portions of almost equal area, both of which slope towards the river. The lowest level in the Division is south of the Ganges, where, in the east, it sinks to 144 feet, though nearer the river it is 160 feet. Following the river towards Patna, the general level rises to 175 feet, and at Buxār, near where the Ganges first touches the Division, to over 200 feet.

North of the Ganges the level rises most rapidly in the west, and the general line of drainage in this portion of the Division is towards the south-east. Towards the Nepāl boundary the elevation rises to between 200 and 300 feet, and in the north-west to between 300 and 400 feet.

South of the Ganges the country rises most rapidly along the river Sone, so that the line of drainage is away from that river, on both sides of it, towards the Ganges, a fact which is made use of in the extensive system of irrigation canals which carry the water of the Sone over the country east and west of it towards the Ganges. In the east of this southern portion of the Division the line of drainage is from south to north until it reaches the depressed tract already referred to, which lies east of Patna city, and is separated from the Ganges by a strip of higher ground. The drainage from the south entering this depressed tract takes an easterly course, generally parallel to the Ganges; the rivers divide themselves into a number of minor channels, and, in the dry season, lose themselves, or are absorbed by irrigation, or find their way into the Sakri river, which joins the Kiāl in Monghyr District.

The level country south of the Ganges and east of the Sone is occasionally interrupted by rocky hills, of which the highest, 1,606 feet, is about 12 miles south of Gāya town. The Rājāgriha hills, which run in a north-easterly direction from Gāya, form, for about 30 miles, the boundary between Patna and Gāya Districts. They seldom exceed 1,000 feet in height, and are clothed with low jungle. Hot springs are common. These hills are interesting as containing some of the oldest memorials of Buddhism, and an isolated hill standing north of the main ridge near the town of Bihār is believed to be one mentioned by a Chinese pilgrim-traveller of the beginning of the fifth century, while several other peaks to the south are mentioned by a Chinese Buddhist traveller of the seventh century.

The whole of the southern boundary is marked by a winding range of hills, which forms the outer edge of the Chota Nāgpur plateau. Peaks frequently rise to near 2,000 feet, and various passes lead to the plains.

The southern portion of Shāhābād District, west of the Sone, is occupied by the Kāimur Hills, which form

SONEPUR FAIR.

Photograph by Bourne & Shepherd, Calcutta.

a plateau having an area of about 800 square miles, and an average elevation of 1,500 feet. These hills descend precipitously to the plains, and wall in the Sone valley on the west. There are several passes leading on to the plateau, which drains itself away from the Sone towards the Ganges in the west. The shallow valleys of this table-land are very fertile.

The Sumeswar range, which extends for about 46 miles along the Nepāl frontier in Champāran District, has an average height of 1,500 feet, the highest point being 2,270 feet. At its eastern extremity is the pass through which the British troops marched into Nepāl in the Gurkha war of 1814-15. From the summit of the Sumeswar pass, which crosses the centre of the range, the great mountains of Dhaulagiri, Dayabang, Gosain Thān, and Everest are visible in clear weather. The tract skirting the base of the range is covered with forest.

The river system of the Division consists of a section of the Ganges about 175 miles in length, the lower courses of its great tributaries the Sone, the Gogra, and the Gandak, and the upper courses of various rivers which join the Ganges in the Bhāgalpur Division.

The Ganges first touches the Division near Chausa, in Shāhābād District, and flows in a generally north-east direction until it receives the *Gogra* from the north-west below Chapra, in Sāran District. It then flows somewhat south of east, receives the *Sone* from the south somewhat above Dinapur, and the *Gandak* from the north opposite Patna. In the dry season its width varies from three-quarters of a mile to about a mile. Its channel is constantly shifting, and islands are formed and disappear year after year. In the rains its stream is many times as wide, and considerable tracts of country adjoining its banks, particularly in the south, are annually flooded. During floods boats can sail from Chapra to near Arrah, a distance of 15 miles, and, between Patna and Hājipur, on the Gandak, there is, during the rainy season, one big river, more than seven miles wide.

The *Gogra* flows from the North-West Provinces, and forms the boundary between them and Sāran District until near its junction with the Ganges. The Ganges used formerly to touch Chapra, but has long deserted it, and the town is now on a channel of the Gogra, while Revelganj, which was founded as a mart at the junction of the two rivers, is now on the Gogra well above the junction. This river is very liable to overflow its banks in the rains, flooding Sāran District, especially when the Ganges is also high and blocks its mouth.

The *Sone* touches the Division at the south of Shāhābād District, and flows north-east, dividing Shāhābād from Gāya and Patna. Its channel is very wide, but, except after heavy rains in the southern hills, when violent floods come down, the stream is only about 100 yards broad, flowing through a waste of sand. An extensive system of irrigation canals distributes water over the northern portions of Shāhābād District and the west of Gāya and Patna, from above a great weir 12,500 feet long, built across the river at Dehri, about 80 miles above its junction with the Ganges.

The Sone has not much value as a navigable river. In the dry season the quantity of water is small, and its floods after rain are excessively violent. Like the Kusi the Sone has been moving west for centuries.

It is mentioned by Megasthenes, the Greek ambassador sent about 300 B.C. by Seleukos Nikator, a successor of Alexander the Great, to Chandragupta, King of Magadha, as flowing into the Ganges close to Patna. Its present course is many miles to the west.

The *Gandak* brings down the drainage of the Himalaya between Dhaulagiri and Gosain Thān, so that this river stands in the same relation to this section of the Himalaya that the Kusi and the Tīsta do to sections further east. It enters the Division at Tribeni Ghāt at the extreme north-west of Champāran District, and takes a course generally south-east to the Ganges opposite Patna. The river is enclosed by protective embankments for most of its course through the plains, and the drainage of the neighbouring country flows away from it.

The *Buri Gandak* rises in the north-west of Champāran District, takes a tortuous but generally south-east course, and, passing into Monghyr District, falls into the Ganges opposite Monghyr.

The *Bāgmati* rises near Khātmāndu in Nepāl, enters the Division in the north of Muzaffarpur District, forming the boundary between that District and Champāran. For some distance its course is parallel to that of the Buri Gandak, and it used to join that river near the borders of Monghyr District, but some years ago it cut across to the Tiljuga, and most of its water now passes into that river.

The *Tiljuga* rises in Nepāl, flows through Darbhanga District, receiving a number of tributaries, and passes into the north of Monghyr District. The navigation of the Tiljuga and other Bihār rivers in their upper reaches is seriously interfered with by the practice of the cultivators of making embankments across the streams in the cold weather for purposes of irrigation. The first flood breaks these down, but the river remains more or less obstructed.

In the part of the Division south of the Ganges swamps or *jhīls* are comparatively few. They are numerous north of the Ganges between the rivers, and particularly in Champāran District. In many cases they mark portions of deserted river channels, and, when this is the case, their shape is often highly curved, and sometimes almost annular.

Crops, Manufactures, Products.—Besides rice, *wheat, barley, maize, millets,* and *pulses* of various kinds are staple crops. Barley and the millets are largely grown as cheap food-crops. *Linseed* and *mustard* are the chief oilseed crops, and the former is exported in great quantities. *Indigo* and *sugar-cane* are grown more largely than in any other Division, while *cotton* and *tobacco* are also considerable crops. Artificial irrigation is practised universally.

The chief manufactures are *opium, indigo, saltpetre, sugar,* and *tobacco*. *Opium* is a Government monopoly. It is grown in the Ganges valley under supervision, and manufactured at Patna. The chief manufacture of *indigo* is in the Districts north of the Ganges, which produce more than three-fourths of the whole out-turn of Bengal. *Saltpetre* is manufactured from the saliferous soil which is common in the four northern Districts. *Tobacco* is largely manufactured in Gāya and Darbhanga Districts. Nearly two and a half million cigars and cigarettes were made in 1892-3.

The Division has practically no mineral wealth.

Internal Communications.—The Ganges is navigable for inland steamers all the year round, and there are regular services between Calcutta, Patna, Chapra, and Revelganj. The affluents of the Ganges from the north are all navigable by country boats of large size. The up-stream navigation of the Gandak is dangerous owing to the rapidity of the current, and only half-loads can be carried going against it.

Photograph by] [*Rev. H. A. Sealy.*

THE SONE CANAL.

The rivers south of the Ganges are of little use for navigation, and, in the dry season most of the water of the smaller rivers is used up in irrigation. The Sone is navigable all the year round for boats of small burthen, and for boats of larger size during the rains. Large rafts of bamboos and other timber are floated down this river to the Ganges. The system of irrigation-canals which takes off from the Sone above the great weir at Dehri is used also for navigation. A main canal branches off west, with navigable branches to Arrah and Buxār, and a main canal to the east, with a navigable branch to the Ganges between Bānkipur and Dinapore. There are other branches for irrigation only, and numerous distributaries over the whole system. The Division is very well supplied with roads. The main roads south of the Ganges are metalled, while those to the north, except in the vicinity of large towns, are unmetalled.

The main line of the East Indian Railway enters the Division from Monghyr District near Mokāmeh, and follows the south bank of the Ganges to Patna. From Patna it makes for the Sone, which is crossed by a lattice girder bridge 4,199 feet long, and it continues almost west across Shāhābād District to Buxār on the Ganges, where it turns south-west and crosses the Karamnāsa river into the North-West Provinces. From Bānkipur there is a branch 57 miles long almost due south to Gāya, and there are short branches from Mokāmeh and Bānkipur to ghāts, or crossing stations in connection with the lines north of the river.

The Bengal and North-Western Railway starts from Semāria Ghāt on the opposite side of the river from Mokāmeh, and runs north-west through Samāstipur, Muzaffarpur, and Motihāri to Bettia. From Samāstipur a branch proceeds north to Darbhanga, and thence east to Kunwa Ghāt on the Kusi, while another branch goes north-west from Darbhanga to Bairagnia on the Bāgmati river near the Nepāl frontier. From Muzaffarpur a branch goes south to Hājipur, crosses the Gandak to Sonepur, and proceeds, with a loop from Sonepur to Pāleza Ghāt opposite Bānkipur, along the north bank of the Ganges to Chapra. A branch goes from Chapra to Revelganj Ghāt on the Gogra, while the main line passes through Siwān to the North-West Provinces. The internal communications of the northern portion of the Division are very complete.

Climate.—This Division, as might be expected from its position, has the lowest rainfall and the driest climate in the Bengal Presidency. The rainfall is highest in the tract of country bordering upon Nepāl, and diminishes as we proceed south. The climate of the cold season is most agreeable, for though the actual temperature is not greatly lower than in the other divisions of the Presidency, the air is much drier. The hot weather temperatures are very high, and, in the Districts south of the Ganges, are markedly higher than in the delta or northern Bengal, and hot winds prevail. Of late years a very bad type of fever, possibly an extension of the Burdwān epidemic, or, as some think, due to the water-logging of the country by the Sone system of irrigation canals, has prevailed in South Bihār, and has quite destroyed the reputation for healthiness formerly possessed by this part of the Division.

Observing Stations in Patna Division.	Average Maximum Temperatures in		Average Minimum Temperatures in		Mean Annual Rainfall in inches.
	January.	May.	January.	May.	
Patna	72·7	99·6	49·9	77·2	43·56
Arrah	73·5	101·6	49·5	77·6	41·94
Dehri	75·0	105·2	52·9	78·8	43·11
Buxār	73·6	101·5	50·4	78·3	39·82
Gāya	75·7	104·1	51·5	78·1	44·05
Chapra	73·4	100·3	50·2	76·8	42·28
Motihāri	73·0	96·7	46·6	73·8	47·37
Darbhanga ...	72·2	95·4	52·1	75·8	48·52

PATNA DISTRICT.

Area: 2,075 square miles. Population: 1,769,004.

TEMPLES AT BUDDH GĀYA.

Patna City, population 165,192, the headquarters

of the Division and the District, is, after Calcutta, the most populous town of the Presidency. It extends, with its western suburb of Bānkipur, where the Government offices and the houses of the Europeans are, for about nine miles along the south bank of the Ganges. It is 332 miles by railway from Calcutta, and 680 miles, by river, from the sea. The city is very ancient, and was described by Megasthenes. Patna was a place of great importance under Muhammadan rule. The town is closely built, with narrow streets, and its general appearance is mean. There are no remains of the old fortifications. Its favourable position at the junction of the Sone, the Gandak, and the Ganges makes it still of great importance as a trade mart. Produce, largely oil-seeds and grain, is collected here from the North-West Provinces and Bihār, and sent on by rail or river to Calcutta; while imports, chiefly cotton goods, rice, and salt, are distributed. The Government manufacture of opium is carried on here. In 1892-3, 24,462 chests were sold, which realised over 306 lakhs of rupees.

Dinapore, population 44,419, the military station of Patna, is six miles west of Bānkipur, between the river and the railway. Dinapore was the scene of the outbreak of the mutiny in this Division in 1857. Three native regiments revolted and made off into Shāhābād District.

Bihār, population 47,723, about 33 miles south-east of Patna, is an ancient city, once probably the capital of the province to which it gave its name. The remains of the ancient fort exist. The place is of declining importance, having neither the advantage of being situated on a navigable river or near a railway.

Rājgir, 13 miles south-west of Bihār, is believed to

Photograph by Bourne &] [*Shepherd, Calcutta.*

OLD GĀYA, FROM THE OPPOSITE BANK OF THE PHĀLGU.

be the site of the ancient Rājāgriha, the residence of

Buddha, and the capital of the kingdom of Magadha. It was described by the Chinese pilgrim-travellers of the fifth and seventh centuries, as are also many other places in the vicinity which are interesting in connection with the early days of Buddhism.

Mokāmeh, a station on the East Indian Railway, 282 miles from Calcutta, is increasing in importance, being opposite the Ganges terminus of the Bengal and North-Western Railway.

Gāya District.

Area: 4,712 square miles. Population: 2,138,331.

Gāya, population 80,383, the headquarters of the District, is situated on the Phālgu river, 63 miles by railway from Patna City. The town consists of two parts: the old town and the new. The old town is the residence of the priests. It is irregularly built on a rocky eminence, and the houses, often two or three storeys high, have very thick walls. The new town, where the Government offices and the houses of the Europeans are, is on level ground on the banks of the river. Gāya is one of the most celebrated places of Hindu pilgrimage, and the whole district is full of places of the greatest sanctity. At Buddh Gāya, about six miles south of Gāya, are ruins of the greatest interest in connection with early Buddhism, whose founder lived here in the sixth century B.C.

Shāhābād District.

Area: 4,373 square miles. Population: 2,063,337.

Arrah, population 46,905, the District headquarters, is situated about 14 miles south of the Ganges and eight miles west of the Sone. It has a station on the East Indian railway. The country north of the town is annually flooded by the Ganges, and the road north to the river runs along a causeway. The smaller of the two houses now occupied by the Judge of Arrah was the one so gallantly defended during the mutiny of 1857 by a few Europeans and Sikhs against the Dinapore mutineers under Kuar Singh. A relieving force from Dinapore, advancing from the river along the causeway road, was disastrously repulsed by rebels concealed in a mango grove below it.

Sāsserām, population 22,713, on the Grand Trunk Road, about 60 miles south of Arrah, is a town of declining importance. It contains the tomb of Sher Shāh, Emperor of Delhi, who was born here. The Kāimur Hills rise precipitously from the plain about two miles south of the town, whence a road leads to one of the most practicable ascents to the plateau.

Buxār, population 15,506, on the south bank of the Ganges, is 43 miles west of Arrah by railway. Here Sir Hector Monro defeated the last independent Nawāb of Murshidābād on the 22nd of October, 1764, and finally won Bengal for the English.

Rhotāsgarh and *Shergarh* are ruins of strong hill-forts on the Kāimur table-land. The former overlooks the Sone, standing on the edge of a sheer precipice of 1,000 feet.

DARBHANGA DISTRICT.

Area: 3,335 square miles. Population: 2, 801,955.

Darbhanga, population 73,561, on the Kamla. Originally a Muhammedan town, it has been the residence of the Māhārājas of Darbhanga since 1762.

The principal features of the town are the Palace and its splendid tanks. It is the largest trade-centre of the District.

At *Pusa*, on the Buri Gandak, in the east of the District, cigars and cigarettes are manufactured in great quantities.

Samāstipur is an important railway junction, and has extensive railway workshops.

MUZAFFARPUR DISTRICT.

Area: 3,003 square miles. Population: 2,711,445.

Muzaffarpur, population 49,192, the District headquarters, is situated on the right bank of the Buri Gandak. It has a considerable river trade. The railway from Bettia here divides, one branch going by Sonepur to Chapra and the North-West Provinces, and the other to Semāria Ghāt.

Hājipur, population 21,487, is situated at the junction of the Gandak and Ganges opposite Sonepur and Patna. The Gandak railway bridge connects it with Sonepur.

SĀRAN DISTRICT.

Area: 2,656 square miles. Population: 2,467,477, or 930 to the square mile.

Sāran is the most densely-populated rural District in Bengal. It is exceptionally fertile, and highly cultivated, and hence, notwithstanding the extreme pressure of the population, the cultivators are better off than in other parts of the Division.

Chapra, population 57,352, the District headquarters, is situated on the left bank of the Gogra, some miles above its confluence with the Ganges. The town lies low, and is subject to inundation during exceptional floods, although protected by embankments. It has a station on the Bengal and North-Western railway, 69 miles from Muzaffarpur junction, and 29 miles from Paleza Ghāt, opposite Bānkipur.

Revelganj, population 13,473, on the Gogra, about five miles from Chapra, was founded by Mr. Revell, collector of Government Customs, in 1788, at the junction of the Ganges and Gogra, and although the port is now some distance above the junction, it is still an important trade mart. Oil-seeds are brought down the Gogra from Oudh in great quantities, and transhipped here into steamers and larger country-boats for conveyance to Calcutta, or to the railway at Patna.

Sonepur, near the confluence of the Gandak and the Ganges, is the scene of a great annual fair, well-known all over northern India.

CHAMPĀRAN DISTRICT.

Area: 3,531 square miles. Population: 1,859,465.

Motihāri, population 13,108, is the District head-quarters, situated on the east bank of the Motihāri Lake, 119 miles from Semāria Ghāt, the terminus of the Bengal and North-Western Railway, opposite Mokāmeh.

Bettia, population 22,780, is the largest town in the District, and the most important trade-centre, and is a terminus of the Bengal and North-Western railway, 27 miles from Motihāri. It is the seat of the Maharajah of the name.

BHĀGALPUR DIVISION

Scale 1 Inch=48 Miles.

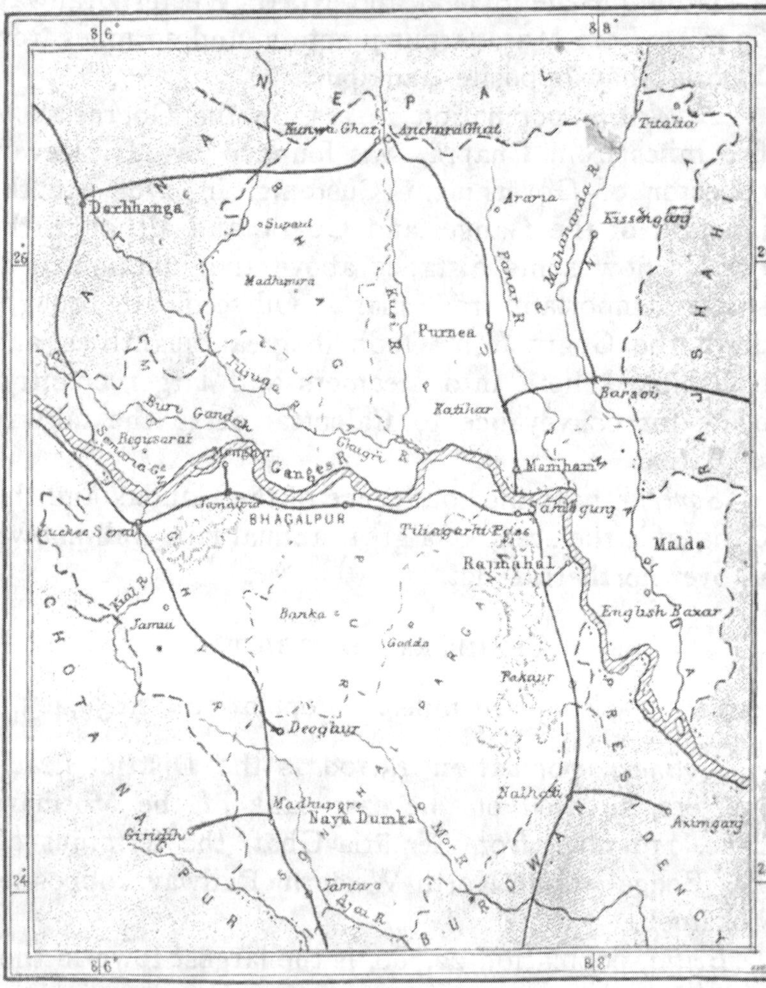

Divisional Boundary

District Boundary

II. Bhāgalpur Division:

Area: 20,511 square miles. Population: 8,582,490.

Districts.	*Area.*	*Population.*
Bhāgalpur	4,226 ...	2,032,696
Monghyr	3,922 ...	2,036,021
Purnea	4,994 ...	1,944,658
Mālda	1,899 ...	814,919
Sonthāl Parganas ...	5,470 ...	1,754,196

Name and Boundaries.—This Division, which takes its name from the town of Bhāgalpur, its administrative headquarters, is the eastern portion of the Province of Bihār. It is bounded on the north by the independent kingdom of Nepāl and Darjeeling District; on the east by the Districts of Jalpāiguri, Dinājpur, and Rājshāhi; on the south by the Districts of Murshidābād, Bīrbhum, Burdwān, and Mānbhum; and on the west by Hazāribāgh, Gāya, Patna and Darbhanga Districts. The Division is divided into five Districts: Bhāgalpur and Purnea to the north, Monghyr to the west, the Sonthāl Parganas to the south, and Mālda to the east, of which Monghyr and Bhāgalpur are intersected by the Ganges.

Size and Population.—The Division is about 194 miles long from north to south, and about 184 miles broad from east to west. Its area is 20,511 square miles, considerably greater than that of any Division of Bengal Proper.

The population in 1891 was 8,582,490, or 418 to the square mile, being least dense in the hill-tracts of the Sonthāl Parganas. More than three-fourths of the whole population are Hindus; a little more than one-fifth are Musalmāns, and about three-quarters of a million belong to aboriginal tribes and faiths, the majority being Sonthāls. As in Patna Division, the condition of the people is not so good as it is further east.

Physical Features.—The general level of the part of the Division north of the Ganges is comparatively uniform, varying between 90 and 160 feet above sea-level. The land lies lowest in the south of Mālda District, near the junction of the Mahānanda river with the Ganges. Here the elevation is 92 feet above sea-level, and there is, as might be expected, a gradual but very slight rise as we proceed up the rivers. The most marked rise is in the north-east of Purnea, where there is a rise from 157 to 297 feet between Kishanganj and Titālia, both on the Mahānanda.

The portion of the Division east of the Mahānanda is similar in character to the adjacent districts of Northern Bengal. Mālda, east of the Mahānanda, is a continuation of the slightly-raised *Barind* country of Dinājpur and Rājshāhi, the soil being a stiff red clay, like that of the western half of Bogra and the Mādhupur jungle in Mymensingh. Purnea, east of the Mahānanda, is part of the depressed area forming Northern Bengal proper, which lies between the Himalaya and the *Barind* country.

The rest of the Division lying north of the Ganges is alluvial plain, intersected by numerous rivers and connecting water-courses, divided from north to south by the river Kusi and a strip of land which the river has overlaid with sand and rendered infertile in the course of its westward movement. This tract is marked by large expanses of grass land extending chiefly north and west from the town of Purnea, which afford

Photograph by] [Kapp, Calcutta.

THE GANGES AND PART OF THE FORT MONGHYR.

pasturage to numerous herds of cattle, and, in the

south, to flocks of sheep. There are also large tracts of pasture land in the marshy part of Monghyr District lying north of the Ganges.

The part of the Division lying south of the Ganges is very different in character. The western portion is a plain divided by a range of hills, which descends to the Ganges at Monghyr, and this alluvial land continues as a narrow strip skirting the river, and liable to annual inundation as far as the boundaries of Murshidabād. Behind this the country rises gradually, and passes by a series of rolling ridges into the jungle-clad hills which are the outliers of the plateau of Chota Nāgpur.

An isolated range of hills thrusts itself forward to the Ganges near Rājmahāl, round the north-eastern base of which the Ganges sweeps south-east to the deltaic plains of Bengal Proper. This range of hills runs, with several breaks, south from the Ganges to the neighbourhood of Bīrbhum. It nowhere rises above 2,000 feet, and its average elevation is considerably less. In the northern portion of the range is a central valley running north and south, about 24 miles long and five miles wide, overlooked by two fine peaks about 2,000 feet high. In the southern part of the range is the peak of Singanmat, a well-known landmark.

The Kharakpur hills, a range of hills running generally north-east, and terminating at Monghyr, are lower, and of different geological character. They abound in hot springs, and, in the south, the range breaks up into conical peaks of no great height.

The hills of the Sonthāl Parganas are generally ungle-clad almost to the summit, but there are numerous passes through all the ranges where good roads can be made. The Tiliāgarhi pass between the Rājmahāl hills and the Ganges used formerly to be of great importance as commanding the military approaches of Bengal Proper.

The river-system of the Division consists of a section of the Ganges about 240 miles in length from where it first touches Monghyr District, to the south of Mālda District, where it leaves the Division, together with its tributaries from the Himalaya on the north, and from the upland country of the south. The general direction of the Ganges is east, with various deviations, until it reaches the Rājmahāl Hills—a permanent barrier to the southward extension of the Gangetic plain. Here the river turns south-east, and this continues the general direction of its main stream through the delta to the sea. The average width of its channel through the Division is three miles, but this is not filled except during the rains, when also portions of the country of varying width on both banks are inundated. It is navigable at all times of the year by river steamers and the largest kind of native boats. The deep-water channel of the river is subject to considerable changes. It has several times changed to north or south of the several islands that lie in the river west of Monghyr. At Bhāgalpur it used to flow directly below the town, and steamers anchored close under the houses of the residents, but at present it flows about midway between its banks, separated from them during the dry season by expanses of sand. Similarly at Rājmahāl a navigable channel formerly flowed directly below the town, whereas the main stream is now three miles distant, and steamers can only approach the town during the rains. The banks vary in abruptness, very much in proportion to the varying incidence of the current and the firmness or friability of the soil of which they are composed.

The Ganges receives from the north a number of important tributaries, navigable within the Division throughout the year by boats of considerable size. The *Buri Gandak* enters Monghyr District from the west, and after a tortuous course, generally parallel to the Ganges, flows into it six miles north-east of the town of Monghyr. The *Tiljuga* enters the Division in the north-west of Monghyr District, and, after receiving several affluents, becomes the *Ghugri*, which flows east through Bhāgalpur District, parallel to the Ganges, and flows into the Kusi a short distance above its junction with the Ganges. These rivers are all connected with one another by cross channels.

The *Kusi* is the most important affluent of the Ganges in the Division. It brings down the whole drainage of the interior Himalaya between Kanchinjinga and Mount Gosain Thān in Tibet. The other tributaries from the north have their origin in the outer ranges. The Kusi is remarkable for the rapidity of its current, the dangerous and uncertain nature of its bed, and, especially, for its constant westerly movement, during which it has devastated large tracts of country in Purnea District. Its present channel is considerably west of that marked on the maps, but of late it has been threatening to break back in a south-easterly direction from near the Nepāl frontier. Where it enters British territory, at the extreme north-east of Bhāgalpur District, it is a large river nearly a mile wide. It here assumes the character of a deltaic stream, and runs a direct southerly course, with many bifurcations and interlacings, to the Ganges. During the rains the Kusi lays many miles of land under water, and pours such a vast quantity of detritus into the Ganges that long islets are heaped up and swept away in a few hours. At this time of year the navigation of this part of the Ganges is very dangerous to country boats.

The *Panār* has its rise in the outer Nepāl ranges, and takes a course generally south to the Ganges. The *Mahānanda* rises in the hills under Darjeeling, and enters Purnea District near Titālia. Its course is south-westerly until it receives the *Kankai* from Nepāl, after which it works gradually east, and, after passing Mālda, joins the Ganges almost due south of the point where it enters the Division.

These rivers in their course through the plains tend to raise their beds by the deposition of silt, so that their banks are sometimes above the level of the neighbouring country. The Kusi at Anchara Ghāt is many feet above the railway. The surface drainage in the western part of the Division is chiefly carried off by the numerous channels which connect the rivers. There are numerous swamps and marshes in the low-lying country between the rivers, of which the largest is Kābar Lake in Monghyr. The general line of drainage is from north to south, with a slight inclination eastwards.

None of the rivers in the part of the Division south of the Ganges are navigable throughout the year—in the dry weather for want of water, and in the rains on account of the violence and uncertainty of their currents. The *Kiāl* is usually navigable during the rains for boats of moderate size for about 20 miles above where it joins the Ganges, 18 miles above Monghyr. The *Ajai*, a tributary of the Bhāgirathi, drains the south-west of Sonthāl Parganas, and then passes into Burdwān Division.

Crops, Manufactures, Products.—Rice, though the largest crop, is not so pre-eminently the staple crop as in Bengal Proper. Large quantities of *wheat* and *Indian corn* are grown, principally in Bhāgalpur and Monghyr Districts. *Barley* is also a considerable crop. *Tobacco* and *jute* are grown in the part of the Division bordering on Northern Bengal. *Opium* for the Patna manufactory is grown in Monghyr. Cocoons of *tusser* silk are largely collected in the Sonthāl Parganas, and some *timber* is floated down in the rains from the forests of the same District. Mālda is celebrated for its *mangoes*. *Siddhi-hemp* leaves are largely imported from Monghyr and Bhāgalpur. *Indigo* is manufactured all over the Division: chiefly in Purnea, Bhāgalpur, and Monghyr. *Silk* is grown and manufactured in Mālda District. Monghyr makes *fire-arms* of good quality. Purnea exports large quantities of *grass matting*. *Country-cloth* is made in Purnea and the Sonthāl Parganas. *Salt-petre* is manufactured to some extent from saliferous soil. *Coal* is found in the Sonthāl Parganas, and in 1892 there were three collieries at work. There are *slate* quarries at Monghyr and *stone* quarries at Rājmahāl.

Internal Communications.—The Ganges and its tributaries in the northern part of the Division are still, notwithstanding the competition of railways, great highways of trade, though not the commerce highways of the country as they are in deltaic Bengal. The Division is fairly well supplied with roads, mostly unmetalled.

The main line of the East Indian Railway crosses the Division from south to north-west, with branches west into Chota Nāgpur. It joins at Luckeeserai, a loop line of the same railway which runs along the south bank of the Ganges through Bhāgalpur and Jamālpur, with short branches to Rājmahāl and Monghyr. North of the Ganges the Northern Bengal Railway runs west from Dinājpur to Barsoi, where a line branches north up the Mahānanda to Kishanganj. At Katihār, 24 miles further west, it meets a line from Manihāri on the Ganges opposite Sakrigali Ghāt, near the Sāhibganj station of the East Indian Railway. This line from Manihāri runs north through Purnea to Anchara Ghāt on the east bank of the Kusi river. It is connected by a ferry with the Kunwa Ghāt station of the Bengal and North-Western Railway, which runs west into Darbhanga, and eventually comes down to the river again at Semāria Ghāt in Monghyr District.

Climate.—The rainfall in the Division, while it continues fairly high in the tract bordering the Nepāl Tarai in the north, diminishes as we proceed west. It is highest in Purnea, and lowest in Monghyr. Purnea and Mālda have a transition climate between the damp climate of Northern Bengal and the dry climate of Bihār, while the Districts west of these have hot westerly winds in the summer months, and a dry, pleasant cold weather. In parts of these drier districts artifical irrigation of the crops is necessary. Purnea District is very unhealthy; malarious diseases are very common, arising from the ill-drained nature of the country, which abounds in shallow swamps and stagnant river courses, generally old beds of the Kusi. Of late years Monghyr and Bhāgalpur Districts have suffered greatly from fever, apparently a form of the epidemic Burdwān fever, which is advancing west.

Observing Stations in Bhāgalpur Division.	Average Maximum Temperatures in		Average Minimum Temperatures in		Mean Annual Rainfall in inches.
	January.	May.	January.	May.	
Purnea	74·7	94·5	47·9	73·6	65·35
Bhāgalpur... ...	74·1	96·3	50·3	75·9	44·84
Mālda	76·2	96·0	50·4	75·3	55·48
Nayā Dumka ...	75·7	98·4	51·2	77·2	57·23

Bhāgalpur District.

Area: 4,226 square miles. Population: 2,032,696.

Bhāgalpur, population 69,106, the headquarters of the District and also of the Division, is situated on a broad and well-raised belt of limestone on the south bank of the Ganges. The town extends along the river for about two miles, and is distant from Calcutta 326 miles by river, and 265 miles by the loop line of the East Indian Railway. There are in the town two monuments to the memory of Augustus Cleveland, who at the end of last century "accomplished," to quote the inscription on one of the monuments, "without bloodshed, or the terror of authority, the entire subjection of the lawless and savage inhabitants of the jungleterry of Rājmahāl."

Monghyr District.

Area: 3,922 square miles. Population: 2,036,021.

Monghyr, population 57,077, the District headquarters, is situated on the south bank of the Ganges, and is one of the most picturesque towns in Bengal. The fort, within which are the public offices and the houses of the European residents, is formed by a great rampart of earth faced with stone, enclosing a rocky eminence projecting some distance into the river, which comes up to the walls on the north. The town is backed by a long range of wooded hills. It was a place of military importance for many centuries, and is still celebrated for its manufacture of firearms. A branch from Jamālpur, on the loop line of the East Indian Railway, runs to the town, which is distant 303 miles from Calcutta. At Jamālpur, population 18,089, five miles south of Monghyr, are large iron-works belonging to the East Indian Railway Company, which employ a considerable number of Europeans. Five miles east of Monghyr are the hot springs of Sitākund. The water is very clear and pure, and its temperature varies between 92° and 138°, according to the season.

PURNEA DISTRICT.

Area: 4,994 square miles. Population: 1,944,658.

Purnea, population 14,555, the District headquarters, is situated on a small river connected with an old channel of the Kusi, which formerly flowed near the town. When this channel was deserted, and began to silt up, the town became extremely unhealthy, and the population has steadily decreased for about 70 years. The health of the European quarter has improved since its removal to higher ground, but the native quarter is still subject to epidemics of fever. The town is 38 miles by railway from Manihāri Ghāt on the Ganges, and has a considerable trade in jute.

Mālda District.

Area: 1,899 square miles. Population: 814,919.

English Bazar, population 13,818, is the head-quarters town, situated on the west bank of the Mahānanda, and protected by an embankment from inundation by the river. It is about six miles below the native town of Mālda, population 4178, which is on the east bank of the river. Both places had formerly thriving silk industries, and still have a considerable river trade in grain. Some miles south of English Bazar are the ruins of Gaur, an ancient capital of Bengal, which extended for about seven miles between the Ganges and the Mahānanda. Towards the end of the 16th century, the Ganges changed its course, and left the city, which then became malarious, and was deserted. The site of Gaur became a tiger-haunted jungle, and its public buildings a quarry for building material; but the jungle is now being cleared, and the land brought under cultivation. Six miles north-east of Mālda are the ruins of Pandua, another ancient capital, which flourished in the 14th and 15th centuries. The seat of the Government was transferred here for a time from Gaur. The ruins were buried in almost impenetrable jungle until their partial clearance by Sonthāl settlers. Here is a partially-ruined mosque, the Adima Masjid (14th century), with nearly 400 domes: a most remarkable example of Pathān architecture, and a popular object of Muhammedan pilgrimage.

The Sonthāl Parganas District.

Area: 5,470 square miles, about the same size as the Chittagong Hill Tracts. Population 1,754,196, of whom 726,284 profess aboriginal religions.